Sanctuary

For Cesca + Phil,

With love,

[signature]

11·20·03

Sanctuary

Steven Schnur

iUniverse, Inc.
New York Lincoln Shanghai

Sanctuary

iUniverse, Inc.

For information address:
iUniverse, Inc.
2021 Pine Lake Road, Suite 100
Lincoln, NE 68512
www.iuniverse.com

Portions of this book first appeared in *The New York Times, The Christian Science Monitor, Reform Judaism,* and the *Scarsdale Inquirer.*

ISBN: 0-595-29577-0 (pbk)
ISBN: 0-595-66021-5 (cloth)

Printed in the United States of America

FIRST EDITION

for my father,

in loving memory

Contents

INTRODUCTION ix

SHAMPOOING THE RINGS OF SATURN 1

THE UNIVERSE OVER BREAKFAST 5

MULTI-TASKING OVER MUSHROOM OMELETS 9

INEFFABLE HEAT 13

BLIND AMBITION 18

SANCTUARY 23

BABY NAMING 26

SANCTITY 29

JANICE 31

OFF GAY HEAD 35

FROM A GREAT HEIGHT 38

SINGING TO THE DEAD 42

ON THE HOME FRONT 46

THE PHONY WAR 50

THE FATE OF OUR MOST CHERISHED WORDS 54

ART AND ALCHEMY 58

IN LOVE WITH SHAKESPEARE 61

NOT JUST ANY PROM 65

RARE SIGHTINGS 69

NEARLY NAKED POWER WALKING 72

COLLEGE BOUND 76

LAST LEAF 80

DRIVING WITH DAVID 83

LOVE AT FIRST SIGHT 88

HOW LITTLE WE KNOW 92

THE DOCTOR IS IN 95

SILENT BEAUTY 99

IF WE ONLY KNEW THEN 103

HEARTACHE AND DELIGHT 107

INTRODUCTION

I have lived in the same village for over forty years, brought here at the age of eight by parents forced, like so many generations of "tempest tossed" immigrants, to flee their homeland in the wake of religious bigotry and war. As I child I knew nothing of their harrowing ordeal, learning of it only years later. But I knew, or rather felt, even before I could articulate the reasons why, that here they had found a home as nurturing and protective as the childhood ideal they had reluctantly relinquished, here they could safely rebuild their displaced lives, here we might all thrive. And in this suburban town half an hour north of New York City we soon found we could express any thought, explore any idea, pursue any dream, quickly coming to feel as much a part of the community as those who had preceded us here by generations.

Gradually this place assuaged the bitter longing of banishment, providing not only the material comforts my parents sought, but the companionship of friends who spoke with the same telltale accent, shared a similar worldview, and harbored similar tales of escape and exile. And it became for me a place of emotional and physical constancy, the solid ground my psyche revisited whenever it required buttressing. Here I was schooled, here I met and married my wife, here we raised our children, and here I have found an environment conducive to the work that has engaged me since I was old enough to hold a pen.

One can write anywhere and at any time; it does not take a village. And yet, for some sensibilities, mine among them, a village helps. Knowing that what one writes will be read not only with interest but some measure of familiarity, even affection, helps to people this solitary endeavor with a vital, nurturing companionship. The very pursuit, the effort to capture and preserve thought, feeling, and experience in words, is valued here. Ever since I penciled and presented my first stories in the nearby elementary school, I have been sustained and encouraged by the generous reception of friends and neighbors. Most of the essays that follow sprang from this very landscape and first appeared in the pages of the village's weekly newspaper.

More than a few authors have remarked that they set to work each day not with a vast audience in mind but just one or two careful readers they hope to entertain and engage with the product of their imagination. I have been fortunate in having a small community serve in that capacity, not only providing the source of many of these thoughts, but embodying everything of greatest moment in my life: family and friends, a rich and treasured past, present inspiration, a sense of the sacred, and the comforting assurance of sanctuary.

SHAMPOOING THE RINGS OF SATURN

Perhaps I should be worried. I'm standing in the shower, eyes closed, water running over my head, unable to recall if I just washed my hair. In all likelihood I finished rinsing out the soap moments ago, but for some reason I'm incapable of focusing on the task, finding that my mind wanders to the farthest reaches of the universe and the deepest recesses of my imagination whenever water runs over my face.

Friends tell me I'm not alone in this, that it's merely a symptom of age, the beginning of that great forgetting that awaits us all. But I prefer to see it as the best possible use of my time. Why linger over the purely reflexive when conscious thought is not needed to complete the job? Better to use that time more productively, to venture out from behind the shower curtain and into the magnum mysterium of unbridled thought and see what riches await.

In fact, I credit the shower with some of my best ideas: it was there I decided to marry, to buy our first house, to give up commuting and find work closer to our newborn twins. It was also there I decided to invest in the dot.com phenomenon, five years too late, to allow my daughter to purchase a second-hand SUV that died three months later, and to reject the first bid on our old house, precipitating a nineteen-month search for a second offer. Okay, so maybe shower thoughts aren't always inspired, but at least I emerge with very clean hair, forgetting most days if I'm just beginning or concluding the process and starting over again, just to be sure.

Some of my friends don't find this condition amusing. It worries them, not so much on my behalf as their own. They too are becoming forgetful, reaching the top of the stairs only to wonder what brought them there, to respond to the voice answering the phone with an embarrassed, "I just forgot who I called," to find themselves unable to name that famous actress, "oh, come on, you know the one, in that classic film, what's it called?"—and rather than just attribute these lapses to the inevitable brain fatigue of age and the impossible density of a half century of information, they see instead the dread specter of Alzheimer's or mad cow disease looming before them.

And perhaps it does loom, though I prefer to blame not bovine spongiform encephalitis or hardening of the arteries but simple saturation and the inevitable shortcomings of any filing system, mental or physical. After fifty years, the cerebrum is bound to grow weary of all the fine distinctions and subtle discriminations it's been called upon to make for decades, all the more so if one continues to read, to learn, to live, cramming yet more information into its fact-burdened lobes. As one prescient observer recently noted, in order to acquire new knowledge in middle age we have to make room for it, jettisoning something from the past, say high school trigonometry, in exchange for learning to program a video recorder.

Two years ago, heeding the advice of the healthy brain movement, I decided to exercise mine more vigorously, adding violin to a small repertory of musical shortcomings. Not long after that, frustrated by a chess defeat at the hands of my nine-year-old nephew (checkmate in four moves), I resolved to brush up on basic strategy. But after realizing I couldn't think more than two moves ahead or remember one move back, I accepted my mediocrity. In similar fashion, I picked up and eventually discarded Japanese brush painting, crocheting, Latin, and basic carpentry. No doubt there will be others, for the process delights me. It's not mastery I seek but acquaintance, like entering a roomful of strangers and emerging with new friends—except where the violin is concerned. I cling to it in the lunatic hope that I might someday produce a noise worth listening to.

It's humbling to realize in middle age how much effort it takes to acquire not only intellectual but physical knowledge, to train hand and brain to work in concert along paths never traveled. We become complacent about skills mastered in childhood, forgetting how much effort they required. Try learning to recite the alphabet backwards to see just how resistant the brain can be to rewiring.

From time to time my children complain of boredom and ask me what they should do with themselves, only to scoff when I suggest taking a walk, reading a book, playing the piano, writing a poem. They want to be entertained not enhanced. I don't mean to sound superior; I remember those moments from adolescence, but blessedly have forgotten how they feel. There aren't enough hours in the day to read all that wants reading, to listen to all that deserves a hearing, to discover all that might delight the eye. This week there's digital photography to explore, a new word-processing program to learn, the vocal artistry of Barbara Bonney to enjoy, along with the movies of Audrey Hepburn, and the nagging urgency to reread *Hamlet*. Next week a new palette of prospective interests awaits.

Can I go to my grave never having learned to compose a waltz, bake edible scones, gone hot-air ballooning, seen St. Petersburg? And there's that manic impulse to record everything of emotional significance in my life, the milestones of my children, the chaos of our times. The world seems infinitely rich, life maddeningly finite. There just isn't time for it all. And I haven't even begun to address all that wants righting in the world, the stubborn resistance of the deplorable, the hazards of zealotry and apathy, not to mention the never-ending need to evaluate and understand change.

So rather than worry about my perpetual lapse of shower memory, I just soap up again, hoping to avoid entrapment in an endless loop of "lather, rinse, repeat." Concentrate, I tell myself, focus on what you're doing. But within moments I'm remembering to pay the Con Edison bill, have the car inspected, call my mother; I'm planning our spring tour of college campuses, which adult school courses to take, wondering what happened to my Beach Boys' albums, the rebate I was supposed to receive for the new computer; I'm climbing Mt. Washington, peering into the Grand Canyon, floating in interstellar space admiring the great gaseous clouds of the Eagle nebula. And then I'm struck by a minor inspiration—after my shower I'll search the attic for our old telescope and show the kids the rings of Saturn.

And suddenly there I am again, water cascading over my face, wondering, "Have I washed my hair yet?" and reaching for the shampoo.

THE UNIVERSE OVER
BREAKFAST

There I was, trying to spread an intractable pat of butter across a rapidly disintegrating slice of toast when my wife suddenly asked: "Does the universe go on forever?" Just like that, no warning, no preparation—metaphysics at 8:15 in the morning, and I hadn't even had my juice yet. Normally I dodge such questions with a deeply reflective, "Who knows." With three small children constantly underfoot, I have trouble enough just seeing my way clear to the end of a sentence, let alone to the outer limits of the universe. In fact, during the last five years, the only remotely ontological discussion we've had concerned the probable life expectancy of our rapidly disintegrating Honda. And I was wrong about that one.

From my five-year-old daughter, I've come to expect such questions, usually on the way home from religious school or in a desperate, last-ditch attempt to postpone her bedtime: "Daddy, where does God live?" "What happens when we die?" "Why is the sky blue?" I can fake the sky one with a smattering of half-remembered high school physics. But the other queries usually leave me stuttering, scrounging around amid the intellectual debris of my adolescence for some dusty philosophical notion that once satisfied a burning curiosity. Like most parents lacking sufficient time to probe the mystery and meaning of life, I've long since grown satisfied with what I call the oatmeal theory of existence: sometimes life is lumpy, sometimes it's smooth—and no one really understands why. But my daughter is not so easily placated, and neither is my wife. She likes her oatmeal smooth and her universe tidy.

Oddly enough, in this particular instance, I felt sufficiently informed to answer. For just the day before, I had read of new astronomical findings at the very edge of the universe, pulsing quasars, or some such interstellar phenomena of the sort that most people, especially those who can't even butter their morning toast, should avoid. But I boldly chose to respond.

"Why only yesterday," I replied, "astronomers in Great Britain reported finding a new star at the edge of the universe."

"The universe has an edge?" she asked in anxious amazement.

"Apparently."

"And then what?" she wondered aloud.

"Don't ask," I replied, having reached the edge of my own severely circumscribed comprehension of the subject. As far as cosmic evolution goes, I'm generally more concerned about the effect three small bladders might have upon our car seats during a two-hour drive to New Jersey than I am about the significance of spectrographic analysis of intergalactic radiation. Call me strange.

But my wife was beginning to worry that my elliptical response concealed not ignorance but secret knowledge of some impending global disaster, some apocalyptic doom lurking in the distant ether. "Don't ask, it's horrible?" she wondered with a look of vague terror, "Or don't ask, I won't understand?"

"Don't ask, I don't understand," I admitted.

"Why? What's out there?"

"The end of time," I replied, "or maybe it's the beginning. I forget." My reading on the subject had not been very thorough. "Does it matter?"

"I'm not sure yet. Tell me about this new star," she insisted. I had never seen her so alert this early in the morning. Cosmology affects people in strange ways.

"Just when they thought they had a fix on things, like how big the universe is and when time began, up pops this interloper a billion trillion light years away, sending them all scurrying back to their calculators. I guess they haven't quite nailed things down yet, off a few billion in either direction, apparently. Must be damned annoying."

"Like trying to account for the missing twelve cents in your bank balance."

"Something like that," I replied, marveling at the human capacity to make concrete the infinitely abstract.

"So now what?" my wife asked. By this time the butter had begun to disappear into a black hole at the center of my cold toast.

"I don't think the findings will have much immediate impact on our lives," I offered.

"But I'd like to know," she pressed. "A person should be familiar with the limits of the universe, don't you think?"

"I suppose," I said distractedly, exhaling over my butter in an effort to soften it.

"And while we're on the subject of unexplained phenomena," she pursued, "why do people yawn?"

That one I fielded without even looking up. "Because they're tired."

"But why? Does it help us fall asleep?" I glanced across the table to see if she was serious. She was. "And why, when someone else yawns, do you yawn too?"

"Because…" I began, and then paused, unable to finish.

"We can send a man to the moon, we can discover light at the very edge of the universe, but no one can explain why we yawn." My wife's voice was filled with ironic incredulity. "And why do people sneeze when they walk out into bright sunlight?"

I shrugged, sensing an impending avalanche of life's insoluble riddles.

"And while we're at it, how come some hard boiled eggs peel easily and others take half the white with the shell? And what good are hiccups? And how come human will precedes human reason, especially in two year olds? And why do things always break the day after the warranty expires? And what about UFOs?"

"All part of the inscrutable mystery of creation, I suppose," I replied, rising from the table.

"Don't go," she pleaded, reaching for my hand. "There's so much we've left unanswered."

"I'm late," I replied, gulping down my juice.

"But what about your toast?" she asked. It lay dismembered across the length and breadth of my plate, mostly crumbs now, surrounding a still rock-hard pat of butter. "What happened to it?"

"Just another one of life's unyielding enigmas, I guess."

MULTI-TASKING OVER MUSHROOM OMELETS

When I looked up from the menu and realized that both twins and my wife had cell phones to their ears, I began to fear for my powers of conversation. Why was the prospect of speaking to someone they could neither see nor, in most cases, hear so much more appealing than addressing their thoughts across the table to me or to each other? What was it about these pocket devices that the whole world found so appealing, prompting millions of otherwise reasonable people to spend a small fortune for the privilege of being interrupted anywhere, anytime, by anyone?

For a dozen years now I have resisted the blandishments of family and friends, refusing to equip my car with a cell phone or hang one from my belt, steadfastly maintaining that the best reason to leave the house is to escape its tyranny. Carrying one around seems as onerous as wearing a court-ordered collar, but then I've never been comfortable making calls, few of the men in my family are. My father used to sit beside a ringing phone insisting, "If you wait long enough, it stops." And it always did.

I feel victimized by its imperial summons, forced to interrupt work, to pause in mid-sentence, to rise from the dinner table, even, on occasion, to step from the shower, dripping with irritation; I feel entrapped by another's impulse, impelled to respond without benefit of adequate reflection or the eye contact so critical to understanding true intent. Perhaps I'm alone in this, or perhaps, as others have suggested, it's genetic. It's not the caller that annoys me so much as the conditions of the conversation. I hear well enough but discovered long ago that hearing alone is not sufficient for comprehension. In order to absorb the full import of another's words I need to be in their presence, to watch mouth and eyes, the tilt of the head, the tension in neck and shoulders. The spoken word is but one part of the total communication and I, for one, simply don't get the message without the other elements. So why compound this discomfort by exposing myself to it wherever I might be?

Several years ago I applauded the advent of email, believing it would herald a more measured and thoughtful means of rapid communication. Ask me by phone if I'm free for lunch and I begin tripping over myself in an effort to juggling all the factors that go into responding to such a seemingly simple question—am I truly free, do I want to be free, what prompted the invitation in the first place, and do I even want to eat lunch that day. My voice becomes halting, I stumble and stammer in an effort to buy time, to think through each concern without wounding the feelings of my caller. Most people, it seems, can navigate these considerations instantaneously but, after roughly fifty years of practice, I'm still as inept as an adolescent suitor.

I watch with amazement as my children juggle not only our two home numbers but their cell phones (equipped with call waiting), moving seamlessly from caller to caller like chess grand masters competing against multiple players simultaneously. If someone so much as enters my field of vision while I'm on the phone, I lose my train of thought, miss what's being said, and have to begin again.

Which is why email seemed such a blessing. I could respond to that same lunch invitation in a timely fashion without alienating the caller with abstracted deflections while weighing the consequences of a simple yes or no. Online I can choose my words carefully, strike just the right tone, exercise thoughtfulness and concision—all of which escape me on the phone.

But for many, email just isn't fast enough. They need to know this instant. An hour from now, even five minutes from now may be too late; an opportunity will have been lost. And like all mail, email is subject to the vagaries of delivery. More than one electronic communication has evaporated in the ether of the Internet, no record of its transmission left behind as evidence of intention. Whether it simply joined those legions of checks purportedly "in the mail," or truly entered some anomalous realm beyond the worldwide web is impossible to say. Nothing, ultimately, is more certain than a live voice on the other end of the phone. The words themselves may be feigned, the emotions concealed, the intentions masked, but there's no doubting their receipt.

Having recovered from my restaurant astonishment, I listened to the several conversations swirling about me, my daughter informing a girlfriend that she had just sat down to lunch, my son congratulating a friend on her new car, my wife checking our phone messages, scribbling phone numbers across a cocktail napkin, all three glancing at the lunch menu. It all boils down to multi-tasking.

We have begun modeling ourselves on our machines. No self-respecting businessman can expect to advance without laptop, Palm Pilot, and cell phone in hand, accelerating his personal data processing capabilities at the rate of the latest silicon chip. I, on the other hand, do best concentrating on one small task at a time. I can't listen to music while writing without losing my train of thought, and am too easily distracted to drive and carry on a faceless conversation. Call my phone or my name, thrust a menu in front of me and I overload; all circuits go down; I must reboot.

My children don't understand the concept of interruption. Like their computers, they simple layer new tasks on top of the old, juggling TV, stereo, phone conversations, call waiting, instant messaging, live friends, and homework concurrently. If they ever feel overloaded they don't admit to it. But perhaps the strain of maintaining so many open circuits accounts for their desperate need to sleep past noon whenever given the chance.

So while I pondered the menu, unable to decide between the chicken Caesar and the mushroom omelet, the kids fired off their orders and checked their messages, eyes glued to the television over the bar. I longed to snatch the phones from their ears, turn off the TV, and enjoy their undivided attention for a moment, but undivided is not a condition they aspire to. Single-mindedness is a shortcoming in their book, a quaint throw back to slower, simpler times before nanoseconds, gigabytes, and megapixels. In an age of digital transmission I'm a pneumatic tube.

Were I to admit any of this to my children they would look at me, as they often do, with the indulgent gaze of the wired for the clueless. It's bad enough that I wear my pants belted at the waist, listen to classical music, would rather read than watch TV; to admit to being so "aurally challenged," so conversationally clumsy, would consign me to realms of the deepest hopelessness in their adolescent minds. As they would say, "The phone rings, you answer it. No biggie." If only it were that simple.

INEFFABLE HEAT

It's ninety-eight in the shade and I'm slowly melting out on the back porch, listening to the distant rumble of thunder and wondering if the storm is headed this way. The temperature hasn't dropped below eighty all week and shows no sign of abating. Upstairs the attic fan whirls helplessly, replacing the stale, super-heated air with fresh, super-heated air. From time to time the roof shudders and cracks, as though shifting restlessly beneath the enormous burden of so much accumulated heat. The hydrangeas are wilting, the impatiens have shriveled, the tomatoes look parched. Any right-minded individual would be holed up in a shuttered, air-conditioned room, sipping something cold, blessing the power company, and eagerly awaiting autumn. But of late I've come to relish such asphalt-melting heat, especially when accompanied by high humidity, crackling afternoon thunderstorms, and the rhythmic crescendo of cicadas. Shirtless, a glass of ice water at my elbow, I sit here reflecting on summer stillness and the sudden sense of the ineffable that surrounds me on such blistering days. The heat feels thick with significance.

Wisely, my neighbors choose this time of year to travel. Except for the town pool, the village seems all but deserted. Ball fields lie browning under the brutal midday sun, playgrounds stand abandoned, their slides and swings too hot to touch, downtown parking spaces go begging, stores sit empty. Even the ubiquitous gardeners and their deafening machines have retreated in the face of the unrelenting heat. Hours elapse without so much as a passing car. But for a single foraging rabbit, a handful of bees, and the undulating waves of cicadas, nothing stirs. This is the season of tranquility and quiet reflection, of indolence, of a sultry saturation—a time for musing on eternity.

Every summer I grow heliotropic, waking just before sunrise to witness the daily miracle of light climbing up out of the earth, coloring the sky, the leaves, the very air, promising another day of withering heat. I walk the quiet, empty neighborhood, thinking about the generations that once occupied these century-old houses. How did they fare in an age before modern refrigeration? Lacking our modern defenses, were they able to armor themselves in other, subtler ways? No doubt, some escaped to the shore or the mountains, but most simply threw wide their windows, hoping to catch the slightest breeze. I sense them sometimes, wiping their foreheads and necks in the shade of street elms, hanging bed sheets on backyard lines to bleach and dry in the searing sun, trimming their lawns with hand mowers, rustling the pages of the evening paper, glancing up the street for the ice man, searching the hazy white sky for signs of change.

What has become of the great weight of thought and feeling that marked their lives, I wonder. How could the world, once so fashioned by their needs, so full of their energy, bear so little evidence of their passing, their thoughts and deeds forgotten beyond a small circle of immediate descendants? A century ago an entirely different cast of characters occupied this small, suburban stage. They too subdued the earth, broadcast their beliefs, reigned supreme. They walked these same streets, suffered the same heat, and marveled at the swift passage of time. With barely a whimper they yielded to a new generation. And yet the sun still rises, chicory continues to blossom blue and spindly beside the curb, bees hover over honeysuckle and lily, and the earth teems with mystery.

In a universe marked by circularity, time seems more a layering than a linearity, an endless returning rather than an infinite spooling out. Despite the future's seeming uncertainty, our destination is plain, the path well worn. Beheld from afar, our lives are no less predictable than the rising and setting sun. Like the light itself, we flourish and fade only to flourish anew. Singular for a moment, we are drawn back into the vastness—just one of the infinite variables in nature's limitless reservoir of creation. To sense that enveloping immensity while alone and adrift in one's small life, to be companioned by history, by God—can there be any greater comfort?

The summer heat has come to feel like the divine fabric out of which our lives are woven. Emily Dickinson seems to have sensed something of the kind. Her poems hang in the shimmering summer air above a heat-intoxicated garden, proclaiming the everlasting link she intuited between heat, hovering bees, and eternity. Walt Whitman glimpsed a similar transcendence in the sweat-stained bodies of laborers and soldiers, office workers and farmers. Shelley spoke of "the white radiance of eternity." Heat lies at the center of the mystery, the source of creation, the quickening that is life. In the almost suffocating press of August humidity, a door to eternity opens, allowing a brief glimpse of all time. That moment is every moment. We stand beside the past, the ether thick with memory, with the simultaneous, with what was, is, and will be.

From my simmering porch I watch the storm-threatening sky begin to brighten. The rumble of thunder grows fainter. There will be no rain today. The fierce heat continues to build until sunset, pressing ever more relentlessly upon rock and shrub, all but declaring, "from this fire you emerged and to it you will one day return." It wrings from me not only sweat but gratitude for its effect upon my imagination. By our inner life we are most nourished, tutored, moved, most comforted. There, through memory or association, all things gain significance—the flight of birds, the greening corn, the upward thrust of fir trees, a word, a gesture—the power to move resident not within objects but ourselves. The pageant of time will play its endless tune, the sun will rise and set, the earth will flower and decay, witnessed or ignored, bursting with implication or devoid of significance as our minds decree. We are free to live within the vortex of this ever-present moment or outside it, susceptible or untouched. Life is either a dull round or a series of electrifying encounters with significance. On this sweltering afternoon the air seems rich with history. A sense of the divine awakens within me. I feel the hot breath of eternity upon my face.

Toward evening the hazy, white sky shades to orange, then magenta, and finally to a twinkling indigo that grows steadily more intense as the earth cools and the summer haze dissipates. For a wider view I leave the porch and walk up the street to the ball field. There the sky is a great black dome that dwarfs the shadowy trees and window-lit houses. I stand in the center of the field and slowly turn. To the north lies Polaris and the Little Dipper, Hercules blazes directly overhead.

If I feel most absorbed by time in the fiery grip of an August afternoon, I come closest to an understanding of the infinite when drawn up among the diamond-blue brilliance of the stars. The night sky, for all its measureless depth and aching emptiness, its manifest challenge to our sense of primacy, comforts me in its fixity. Released from the blinding tyranny of daylight, I behold a wholly different order. Casting my eyes heavenward, I join every ancient star-gazer who puzzled over his importance amid the dark and twinkling void. There, laid bare for all to behold, lies the comforting blackness that engenders all light, the featureless face of God, immutable, embracing, boundless, benign.

The grass grows damp underfoot as the air cools. I clutch my arms to my chest. After temperatures near one hundred, eighty feels cold. Somewhere up the street a dog barks; overhead a lone jet negotiates the stars. I return through a bubble of receding crickets. My wife sits on the back porch under a lamp reading the paper.

"Is the moon out?" she asks.

"Not yet."

I take my place beside her. We have lived in each other's affections for over thirty years. This is where the strength to face eternity comes from, this complex union of love and trust, this shared commitment to discover the sacred in our midst.

The garden is invisible now beyond the screens, but the air is alive with the vitality of summer darkness. The crickets grow bold, the fireflies flicker. We seem completely alone, the first and last couple on earth, the center and rim of the universe. And for just a moment that universe seems gifted to us.

The first faint aura of the rising moon appears through the trees. I switch off the lamp to better witness its ascent into the blue-black sky, a dusky yellow face, the mirror of mankind, assuming its deathless station among the stars.

BLIND AMBITION

On the coldest night in nearly a century, with hurricane-force winds howling across the Mt. Washington summit and chest-high snow drifts clogging the high passes, two young men began an ill-fated ascent of the Presidential range, determined to complete the sixteen-mile traverse during one of the worst storms on record. Carrying only light provisions and no tent, they quickly discovered that progress in the teeth of the gale was punishingly slow and exhausting. After twenty-four brutal hours, the weaker of the pair gave up the struggle and climbed into his sleeping bag to die while his companion pressed on to the weather observatory at the summit of Mt. Washington, hoping to summon help. The next morning a rescue squad battled its way up the still raging mountain to the corpse. Along the way, one of the mountaineers inadvertently knocked the goggles from his face. In the arctic cold his eyes instantly froze shut. He had to be led down the treacherous mountainside blind.

With the exception of such emergencies, I had never heard of blind mountaineers until I encountered one on the shoulder of Mt. Washington one windy afternoon in late May. I was headed down off the summit when I spotted a heavily ladened hiker and dog approaching from the south. I didn't notice the white cane or the special harness particular to Seeing Eye dogs until I was about to pass them. The young man was feeling his way along the Crawford Path, fighting a stiff westerly wind that repeatedly blew him off the trail. I watched in drop-mouthed amazement as he progressed, stumbling repeatedly, his arms jerking forward each time to break a possible fall. I trembled for him. How had he gotten this far? How would he make it back down the treacherous mountainside?

I understood how a cane might alert him to impending danger on an otherwise smooth surface, a city sidewalk, say, or a hallway. But on a rock-strewn trail over roots and boulders, across streams and narrow ravines, a trail that was never smooth, that exhibited more variety in three feet than a city street did in three miles, how much help could a cane provide? Still, he came on, pausing frequently to catch his breath, reaching down to pet his golden retriever, planning his next footstep. How, without seeing the trail blazes and cairns, did he keep to the path? Below the summit, through the forested flanks of the mountain, the trail was generally apparent underfoot, a narrow swath cut through underbrush, boulders, and trees. But above tree line one had only an occasional white or blue blaze painted on stones to indicate the way over a vast and rocky plateau where a wrong turn could be fatal.

As we neared each other, the blind hiker set his heavy pack down and began foraging through it with both hands. He removed a small bowl then returned to the pack for water, all the while talking to his dog. After filling the bowl, he took a drink himself, then rummaged around for a granola bar while his companion quickly lapped up the water. Hearing footsteps, the hiker turned in my direction.

"Beautiful day!" he said between bites.

The wind had grown colder during the last hour, but the sky was cloudless. I wonder if he knew that. "How are you managing?" I asked, unable to restrain my curiosity. I couldn't conceive of walking even two steps across such a treacherous landscape with my eyes closed.

"Fine," he replied, "and you?"

"Forgive me, but if I can be of any help?"

"Nope. We're doing okay," he insisted. "Lakes of the Clouds up ahead?" He turned his sightless eyes in that direction. How did he know which way to turn?

"Are you spending the night at the cabin?" I asked.

"If I get there in time. I made a reservation. If not, I'll manage." A bedroll, sleeping bag, and tent were strapped to his towering pack.

"I left there about an hour ago," I said, assuming that would cheer him. "It's not far."

"Then I should make it before dark."

"Oh, long before," I assured him. "It's not more than two miles away."

"With all the obstacles up here, I've got to go slow. A mile takes me about two hours." At that rate, the sixteen miles I'd traversed since morning would require three or four days.

"Where are you coming from?" I asked. He mentioned a cabin a few miles south, deep in the national forest. "I mean where did you start originally?"

"Kinsman Notch."

"You've walked all that way alone?" I blurted out. He'd covered some of the most rugged terrain in the White Mountains.

"With Lance," he said, indicating his dog.

"But how?"

"One small, wobbly step at a time," he said smiling.

"And how far are you going?"

"We'll see. I had visions of making the Maine line, but it's slower going than I expected. At this rate I'll settle for Madison Hut and Pinkham Notch."

"You're planning on doing all the Presidential peaks?" I asked in disbelief. As tough as the footing was south of Mt. Washington, it grew infinitely worse to the north, eight long miles of wearying stone dancing under the best of conditions. The landscape was exactly as Thoreau had described in his traverse of Mt. Katahdin: "a vast aggregation of loose rocks, as if some time it had rained rocks, and they lay as they fell on the mountain sides, nowhere fairly at rest, but leaning on each other, all rocking stones, with cavities between, but scarcely any soil or smoother shelf." To traverse those fields with open eyes was hazardous; to do so blind—mile after pitiless mile—seemed impossible.

"It's extremely rocky up ahead," I cautioned.

"I know. I read up on it. I'll have to go real slow. These'll help." He pointed to a pair of thick ski gloves strapped to his backpack then patted his knees, revealing basketball kneepads beneath his sweatpants.

"You're amazing!" I blurted out.

"Or stupid," he countered, reaching for and finding Lance's head again.

I had dozens of other questions, but he turned around to stow his water bottle and Lance's bowl, then shouldered his heavy pack, grabbed his cane, and said, "I've got to keep going or I'll never get there."

"Good luck," I said.

"Same to you."

I watched his first tentative steps. He stumbled, caught himself, laughed, then continued on, feeling his way, tapping, pausing, deciding, then moving ahead slowly, cautiously, determinedly. Lance walked alongside panting patiently, somehow keeping them both on the faintly marked trail.

I climbed mountains for the view, to indulge my sight, to feel the exhilaration that comes from high prospects. I loved the steady climb, the uphill exertion, but it was the promise of endless vistas that impelled me. Would I hike if I could not see? It was beyond my imagining. A different world exists for the sightless, we're told, a world of heightened senses, of highly refined touch and smell, of acute hearing. And just as the mountains provide heightened encounters with the pleasures of sight, so it does, perhaps, for the other senses as well. I had not, until that moment, thought much about them, but the well-tempered hiker encountered a wealth of rich woodland smells and an endless variety of sounds: birdsong and squirrel chatter, rustling leaves and sighing wind. And underfoot and in hand the ever-changing contours of the trail, the smooth and ragged bark of tree limbs and trunks, the prick of pine needles, the balm of maple leaves.

Some hike to lose themselves among the trees, others to climb above them. Everyone on the shoulders of Mt. Washington experiences the thrill associated with its unpredictable alpine climate. Whatever else the blind hiker sought, his pleasure in the journey and in his proximity to peril seemed no less than my own, perhaps greater. For him, it was not the destination that mattered but the journey, the ongoing encounter with the new, the threatening, the just conquered. Though he might stumble, it was that very danger that drew him on, as it drew me, challenging us both to widen our cordon of safety, to venture into unfamiliar territory, climbing higher, steeper, further, exhilarated by mere survival. Sightless or seeing, we are forever changed by the journey.

SANCTUARY

My father never thought of himself as a refugee. He never suffered sudden expulsion, stateless wandering, DP camps, was spared the midnight arrest, the hastily packed suitcase, the barred, indifferent gate. Nevertheless, like so many of his generation, he died thousands of miles and worlds away from the place of his birth, forced by the politics of hate to flee a malignant homeland and resettle on more benign soil. Affluence and foresight helped ease his passage but not even a first-class steamer ticket could efface the terrible fact of his repudiation. His Jewishness had made him a pariah throughout Nazi-occupied Europe and, had it not been for his father's prescience and planning, he might very well have ended up in the sealed cattle cars destined for Auschwitz. Instead he landed in New York and for the last forty-one years of his life in a small suburb once stigmatized for its effete anti-Semitism. He delighted in reciting the old comic definition of the Yiddish term *farblunget* (hopelessly lost)—a kosher butcher in Scarsdale—having lived to see not only kosher butchers in town but an entire culture influenced and enriched by his compatriots, the very people Hitler had spurned.

My father was a quiet man, almost reclusive in his later years, given to photography and orchid cultivation, computers, classical music, and science fiction. He was never a joiner, eschewing country clubs and civic organizations, public worship and patriotic celebrations. Hounded from Germany, Holland, and France, he never quite shook the gnawing dread that such anti-Semitic fervor might one day grip this nation as well. His father had made a name for himself in Germany, landing near the top of Hitler's hate list of Jewish industrialists. In response, my father cultivated anonymity and practiced a quiet philanthropy, frequently reminding his children of the poisonous power of envy. Nothing good ever came of catching the public eye, he insisted. Scarsdale offered him exactly the refuge he sought—quiet, secluded, respectful of his privacy, and tolerant of his political, social, and religious beliefs. He never wanted to live anywhere else.

When we first moved to the village in the summer of 1960, I too felt something of my father's relief. We had come from a nearby town where, as the only Jewish family in the neighborhood, we had suffered occasional anti-Semitic taunts and even a broken window punctuated by shouts of: "Dirty Jews! Get out!" We endured no such derision in our new home. Still, it was hard to shake the cautions instilled by the war. So my father continued to keep largely to himself and, like his father before him, quietly prepared for future flight. Real estate, he knew, could be confiscated, furnishings were not easily transported, paper currency might be rendered worthless by hyper-inflation, as it had been in Weimar, Germany, but gold coins, he told us, would always retain their value, securing food and shelter in an emergency. He would not be caught unprepared.

Blessedly, America surprised him, and eventually he all but ceased his coin collecting. The expectation of assault and the impulse to flee gradually waned. He no longer talked of the inevitable pogrom that would be visited upon American Jews. In time he could no more envision leaving Scarsdale than he could imagine resettling in Berlin. The village had become his home, the place he inhabited longer than any other, embodying everything America stood for in the eyes of the refugee: a safe haven free of overt prejudice, protective of its young, of the right to privacy and independence, devoted to cultivating the life of the mind and rewarding ambition. Upon such a foundation almost anything could be built, including a new faith in mankind, or at least in the saving power of American moderation. Democracy, he discovered, was a powerful governor of extremism.

By the time of his death, my father had dispersed his collection of coins as gifts. They had proved unnecessary. The only prejudice he had fled in his four decades here was the one he brought with him. America, he realized, would not betray his trust, and Scarsdale would never make him feel anything but welcome. His neighbors would not hound him from his house as they had in Berlin, the government would not seek his expropriation and death. This was his home as no other village or city in the world had been, the place that had provided not only asylum but full equality. Here he was not refugee but citizen. Religion would never disqualify him, never stigmatize him, never endanger him. Nazism would never flourish here. Good fortune had landed him in this most democratic of towns and he was forever grateful for its existence.

My father's last wish was to die in the house that had sheltered him for four decades. And with the help of hospice care, family, and friends, he was able to do just that. Here he had found a refuge from hate and here he died a death denied so many of his German-Jewish peers, quietly in his own bed, surrounded by his family and the town that had offered him sanctuary.

BABY NAMING

Fifty years after she died, my sister was named. And with that naming my mother felt a long and lingering regret begin to ease and the healing promised by time finally take root. Five decades earlier well-meaning relatives had counseled her against formal ceremonies of burial and mourning, believing that such rites would only amplify her grief. Jewish law seemed to support their position: a stillborn child, a child unnamed, even one that survived only a few weeks, did not require the traditional rituals of mourning. Better to get on with life, to put the past behind her as quickly as possible and have another child.

To her everlasting regret, my mother heeded their counsel. She was young, married little more than a year, and terribly disoriented by her recent arrival in America. In a few short months her life had been turned upside-down. She and her parents had only just emerged from the Holocaust, shaken but intact. Raised for her protection in the Lutheranism of her mother rather than her father's Judaism, she had converted on the eve of her wedding and was just beginning to adjust to her new life as a Jewish wife in post-war Europe when the sudden death of her father-in-law catapulted her across the Atlantic into a new and bewildering world. Surrounded by new relatives in deep mourning in the midst of an alien culture and language, she suddenly discovered she was pregnant. When the time for her confinement arrived, a terrible series of medical misjudgments precipitated the stillbirth of her first child. When my mother awoke from her drug-induced nightmare, her daughter was gone and the relatives hovering around her, all still aching from their own recent bereavement, urged her to let the child go. She never set eyes upon her, never held her, never said goodbye.

For twenty years my mother kept that loss a secret. Four more times she gave birth, hoping on each occasion to recover the daughter denied her, but son followed healthy son; there were to be no more daughters. It wasn't until my sixteenth year that I learned about my stillborn sister. Unbeknownst to us all, my mother had continued to mark the day of her birth and death, silently, privately, counting the years, picturing her as a little girl, an adolescent, a young woman. In all that time she had never lit a candle or said a prayer within our hearing, but every year on the anniversary of that indelible loss, she considered how much life had gone unlived, how different her world might have been. Year after year she lamented her failure to embrace her dead child, to see her just once and then to bury her with the rites normally accorded the dead. That there was no gravestone to visit, no exterior geography of mourning, left her perpetually locked within her grief.

As I became more aware of her suffering I suggested she erect a memorial stone among the graves of my grandparents, but my mother demurred. It seemed too public an admission of a wound unhealed. She would continue to mark the death in private, silently hoping that the relief her sons had not been able to provide might eventually come through her grandchildren. And, in time, it did, at least in part. The year my sister would have turned thirty-five my daughter was born. From the moment my mother learned of her birth, the long-deferred healing began. Though she continued to mark my sister's anniversary, she finally could enjoy the companionship of a daughter and incarnate a lifetime of wishes. They grew wonderfully close.

And then, finally, as the fiftieth anniversary of my sister's death approached, my mother declared herself ready to acknowledge her publicly, to observe her yahrzeit as she had observed those of her father and, more recently, her mother. Until that moment I had never asked my sister's name. My mother had always referred to her simply as her "first pregnancy" or as "your sister." But in her heart she had always thought of her by name, the name she had chosen with my father when they first discovered their expectancy. Now finally she spoke it and in doing so seemed to confer new life, to grant to her daughter an identity that had, until then, hovered just beyond reach, disembodied for lack of something as simple as a name. I asked our rabbi to add her name to the yahrzeit list and the week of my sister's fiftieth birthday, my mother and I stood among our fellow congregants and heard it spoken aloud. And then, for the first time, I recited *kaddish* for my sister.

That loss can never be effaced; my sister will always abide within my mother's heart as a source of sorrow and yearning. But named, she seems to have become as much loving memory as longing, the living impulse that impelled my mother to have son after son. But for my sister, the four of us might never have come to be. In a sense, we owe her our lives.

When I again asked my mother if she wanted to erect a stone for her daughter, she thought long and hard and finally decided she no longer needed such a place to mourn. Not only had the pain diminished; not only had she discovered some measure of peace; but she felt now that the most fitting memorial was her own heart. There her daughter's name had been engraved for half a century. "When you lay me to rest," she said, "put her name beside mine on a single stone."

When that day comes we will do so.

SANCTITY

One by one the cars inch forward as we drop our children off at the high school—a daily ritual—only this morning the line moves more slowly. For once, no one honks impatiently. We wait silently, almost deferentially, as fathers and mothers hug their teenage sons and daughters one last time before letting them go off to class. Through the windshield I watch a mother lean over and take hold of her son's hand, pulling him back a moment to kiss his forehead. I lay my hand on my daughter's knee and murmur, "I love you. Be safe."

What normally passes as mindless routine is tinged today with great sadness and a throat-catching gratitude: fifteen parents have just lost their sons and daughters in a barrage of pipe bombs and gunfire at a high school in Littleton, Colorado. It could have happened here, to our children. We might have been the ones behind police barricades waiting for the awful tidings. But we were spared; for the moment our children are safe. But what about tomorrow? Is Littleton so different from our town? What homicidal undercurrent of hate lies waiting to erupt in our own neighborhood?

I watched the news in stunned horror, tears coming to my eyes every time a grateful parent ran to meet a rescued child, shuddering at the fear-glazed eyes of parents not yet reunited with their children. I slept fitfully, awakened repeatedly by the remembered voices of terror-stricken teenagers who had come face to face with a motiveless malignity so callous it had mocked their pleas for mercy and murdered their friends at point-blank range.

What is one to do with such scenes, with the devastating realization that our most basic belief in the sanctity of human life is not shared by our neighbors? How is one to contend with the knowledge that our children are not safe in the very places charged with fostering that sense of sanctity?

"Why is this happening?" my daughter asked, watching teenagers dressed just like her racing from their school, from what should have been a place of sanctuary not mortal danger, hands over their heads as though prisoners of war—innocent victims pursued by madmen, their trust shattered, their childhood abruptly and terribly terminated. Why, indeed! The endless parade of violence marches on in this genocide-intoxicated century and we watch powerless and benumbed. Sanctity of life! Where do we find it? When what passes for art in our culture is so infested with violence—our movies, television, music, literature—is it any wonder that on our streets and in our schools we see the dark current of our fatal preoccupations made manifest? Every witnessed act of violence corrupts, pollutes, and debases. Put guns within easy reach of a society that has lost its sense of the sacred, that equates automatic weapons fire with stress-relief, and the stage is set for carnage.

I had no answer for my daughter's pain-filled cry. Worse still, I could not assure her or myself that what happened at Columbine could not happen here. The insidiousness of the violence with which we entertain ourselves, infects us in terrible and unanticipated ways. Columbine has become the innocent victim of self-hate, yet another civil war in a world wracked by internecine violence, one more eruption of the terrible undercurrent of hatred that lies festering in the human soul.

JANICE

Janice's death was different, more dislocating at first, then oddly less final. I had buried friends and relatives before but never someone so young, never someone whose creative spirit seemed so inextinguishable. When she died I seemed to discover loss as if for the first time, suddenly realizing what it means to make a call that will forever go unanswered, write a letter that will remain unread, tender an invitation that will never be accepted.

If we are most human in moments of empathic communion, during those singular instances when we share affection, conviction, even loss, then Janice's death left me greatly diminished. Suddenly an essential link with humanness was severed, a rare and beloved destination lost. No longer would I be able to discover my own feelings embodied in her elegant, impassioned prose, no longer arrive at an understanding of my own thought through encounters with her suffering. In her company one felt a singular sense of enlargement, of being in the presence of life's conflicting forces—love and hate, condemnation and forgiveness, weakness and strength, acceptance and denial—at precisely that point where discord becomes communion, contradiction congruence. Janice possessed a preternatural understanding of the human heart—and now she was gone.

When I first met her in the fall of 1993 she was already dying, dying and yet more alive than anyone I knew. Not yet thirty and already seven years infected with the HIV virus, she walked into my classroom and began to read a chapter from what would become her tribute to the human spirit, her memoir, Sarah's Song. I had witnessed the deaths of many from the disease by then, but always from the safe distance of casual acquaintance. Until that moment I had never been in such close proximity with its daily trials, never truly understood its costs, never looked across a narrow table into the unblinking eyes of someone so young laboring under a sentence of death. I listened in shock as she detailed the soul-wrenching first days of her discovery, her desperate cries for salvation, the agonizing choices she faced. My mind reeled: how to respond? I took refuge in a seeming professionalism, reminding myself and the other students in the writing workshop that, as compelling as Janice's personal drama was, we were there not to probe further into her life but to address the particulars of her prose. Janice's relief was palpable: she sought constructive criticism not commiseration. At a time when HIV infection was routinely concealed, she and her husband had decided to disclose their illness, to make of their suffering a crusade, to try to shift the communal response from censure to compassion. They sought, in her words, to attach a human face to AIDS.

For the next three years I found myself repeatedly rendered speechless by her unflinching depictions of the physical agony, emotional torment, and transcendent faith that accompanied her and her husband's gradual acceptance of their fate. During her ten-year ordeal she was spared no suffering. From the first nausea-inducing encounter with her own mortality at the hands of indifferent lab technicians to the womb-wrenching realization that she would forever remain childless, from her vigil over a disease-wracked husband to her premature widowhood, from the tortures of experimental drugs, the loss of hearing and balance, the onset of blindness, the never-ending sorrow of burying countless friends and acquaintances similarly infected to the appalling insensitivities of a culture still intent on blaming the victim—all these she endured, all these she recorded, all these she miraculously transformed into art.

In the beginning we worked together, week after week, as she hurried to record all that had been and all that was then unfolding—the temptations of despair, the discovery of new hope and strength, and the sudden, terrible deterioration of her twenty-nine year old spouse. Until that moment she had assumed she would not live to see the completion of her work, that her book would end only with her own death. So long as she possessed the strength to record her experience she would never be able to bring it to completion. But with the death of her husband, the work became a memorial. She rushed to complete it even as she prepared to bury him, her art becoming transcendent within the dreadful crucible of those days as she threw off the shackles of death and wrote clear of mortal fear or spiritual doubt, recording the clarified promptings of a seared, accepting heart.

During this period Janice became a frequent guest in our house. My wife discovered someone of rare compassion in whom she could confide; our children learned that AIDS does, indeed, possess a human face, one they grew to love; and I found not a student but a colleague who enjoyed discussing the business of writing. Janice became an important intellectual and emotional address for us all, someone with whom we could share everything of consequence in our lives, just as she shared her trials and triumphs with us. Even as she grew noticeably frailer, struggling with failing hearing and sight, with uncertain balance, landing repeatedly in the hospital in an effort to stabilize her volatile medications, even as she came back, as she later reported, from the brightly lit precincts of death itself, we continued to believe she would endure, that we would always have her to confide in.

But ten years at the frontiers of experimental medicine, ten years of being brought repeatedly to the brink of annihilation in an effort to destroy the virus within, had exhausted her dwindling resources. A blood transfusion tainted with hepatitis wrestled her to earth and after a three-week battle, claimed victory. Three days later we accompanied her to her grave, said a final goodbye, and returned home to an emptier house, to emptier lives.

Yet within days an astonishing transformation occurred. Though we could no longer pick up the phone or a pen, no longer set a place for her at the table, we continued to feel her presence, continued, in our separate ways, to commune with her, ask her advice, measure our actions against the standards she had unintentionally set. What mourning we did was blessedly brief, not because we had to get on with our lives, but because we felt less a sense of loss than of transformation, as though Janice were simply out of immediate touch but still actively resident in our hearts. It was a stunning discovery, and not confined to our household. Janice's parents and sisters spoke of her continued presence in much the same way, so did many friends. For the first time I experienced death not as loss but transfiguration. Where before she had been outside and beyond, now she dwelt within, a continual comfort and inspiration, a companion of the heart.

Since her death, new treatments have begun to hold out the hope that AIDS may one day become as manageable as diabetes, a chronic but not necessarily mortal affliction. With each new discovery, something like a pang of regret reverberates in our hearts—if only Janice had lived this long, how much longer she might have survived. But she had defied the odds, outliving almost everyone infected when she was. Her courage in the face of experimental therapies helped chart the course that now helps so many. No, we don't long to have her back in the flesh enduring still more trials—she suffered enough. We long only for her unexampled love of life, and that we can summon whenever we need to.

OFF GAY HEAD

The children swam just off shore, splashing and shouting and bobbing on the gentle surf, occasionally venturing too far out to sea only to be called back by anxious parents. We sat in the sand watching their silken, seal-like heads and beyond them the distant recovery ships off the southwest tip of Martha's Vineyard. It was Tuesday, July 20, the thirtieth anniversary of man's first footstep on the surface of the moon, and the fourth mournful day of the search for the wreckage of John Kennedy Jr.'s private plane. The ships might have been fishing vessels or coast guard cutters, the kind of boats one expected to see from that beach near Gay Head light. From where we sat it was impossible to tell. But we knew, the whole world knew.

The children, however, took no notice. The name John Kennedy meant nothing to them, neither did the sudden crush of reporters. Only the waves and the sea-smoothed stones captured their attention. But we could not avert our gaze. There, just seven miles out to sea, lay the late president's son and with him not only his wife and sister-in-law but the tender regard, perhaps even the hope, of a generation that for thirty-six years had felt cheated of promise. How different the history of the second half of this century—our century—would have been but for that day in Dallas, we often thought, and how much better. Vietnam and Lyndon Johnson might both have evaporated by mid-decade, so too Richard Nixon and Watergate, undoubtedly Ford and Carter, and perhaps even Reagan, Bush, and Clinton. Who can say what course our nation might have pursued? Most certainly it would not have been, could not have been, the present one.

Of course nothing and no one could turn back the clock, revive the dead, slay the demons unleashed by assassination, but the president's son helped to ease the ache, declaring by his very existence that all had not been lost that terrible November day, that an heir remained, not to incarnate those shattered dreams—he did not possess his father's fiery political ambition—but simply as a symbol of mercy, of grace, of continuity. The political vision of the president had died with him and five years later with his brother Robert, but not the blessings of posterity. As mourners take comfort in the presence of swaddled and cradled new life in a house of bereavement, so the nation took comfort in John and Caroline, a comfort both personal and political, a comfort unique to the singular role played by the Kennedys in American political and cultural life and the rare position they held in the American psyche.

And now we sat in vague mourning, waiting for word from the recovery ships, our own children floating on the same waters that had claimed the country's surrogate son and heir to an age of promise, an age free of the cynicism and contempt that indelibly marked post-Watergate political life. The day burned on, lobstermen steaming by on their way into Menemsha harbor where rows of cameramen and satellite trucks awaited word from the sea, sailboats tacking across the sound, gulls floating overhead, the waves rolling inexorably up the beach. On the cliffs above, the Gay Head light flashed its red and white beacon keeping fog-bound ships safe from harm—but not that one hapless Piper Saratoga. The hot summer haze that claimed three lives transformed the distant ships into a quivering, milky mirage. The sun grew crimson as it dropped towards the Elizabeth Islands. Though the hour grew late, we lingered, unwilling to relinquish this final connection to the past, to loose these bands of memory and longing and hope.

Finally the children returned to shore and collapsed on the beach, exhausted, ravenous. We wrapped them in towels as the shadows lengthened and the air began to cool, gathered up sand toys, beach chairs, and sandals, then paused for one last look out to sea. The ships' lights burned like tiny earthbound stars just above the calm surface of the sea. The children puzzled over our faces. What were we looking at, they asked. Just those distant boats, we replied, and our vanished dreams.

FROM A GREAT HEIGHT

There were no details at first, only the sorrowful news that an old friend had died under uncertain circumstances while climbing in the Swiss Alps, leaving behind a widow, two grown children, and an unrealized dream. A subsequent exchange of letters brought only more questions. In the end I had to content myself with knowing only that there had been a terrible accident somewhere on the east face of the Matterhorn and that Rony was dead.

I had met him fifteen years before while hiking the remote reaches above Zermatt. For ten days he led a group of us through a landscape of lush alpine meadows and lunar moraines shadowed by the soaring gray beauty of the Matterhorn. I found the pull of the daunting, deadly peak all but irresistible, awaking each morning before dawn to watch the dark triangular summit catch the first amber light, captivated by the constant play of clouds clinging to its craggy flanks. Just how difficult was it to climb, I wondered. "With three days for training and two for the ascent," Rony replied in his thickly accented English, "I'll get you to the top." Just five days? Me? On the summit of the Matterhorn? The thought was intoxicating. Perhaps it wasn't as dangerous as it looked. I stood on our hotel balcony as the last red rays ascended the northwest ridge, the most common route to the summit, picturing myself clinging to those jagged rocks. The light lingered a moment on the peak then leapt into the watery blue sky, leaving behind the portentous grey monolith, darkly visible long after midnight. Five days could bring me to that peerless height, as close to the top of the world as I was likely to get, just five days and Rony's skilled and cautious hands—if I had the nerve.

Until that moment I had never seriously considered such a climb, thinking such feats the province of dedicated mountaineers, not casual hikers. But as the week's itinerary brought us ever closer to the snow-covered shoulders of the great limestone colossus, and as I watched the rugged, unshaven climbers return to the village each evening, ropes, crampons, and ice axes strapped to heavy packs, unmistakable expressions of mastery upon their deeply tanned faces, I wondered, could I really challenge every assumption of comfort and safety that had ruled my suburban life and leap, however briefly, into an altogether different realm, one as matchless and unforgettable as the mountain itself?

Thousands before me had responded to a similar impulse. It was, after all, how Rony and his elite colleagues, the Zermatt mountain guides, made their living. He had summited hundreds of times. His uncle, the village's best-known guide, had celebrated his 90th birthday with a climb to the peak, becoming the oldest man to do so. On summer mornings, as many as two hundred climbers set out before dawn to scale the 14,500 foot mountain, but it was no less dangerous for its popularity, claiming the lives of both skilled and unskilled climbers with pitiless regularity. Yet Rony assured me he would be able to see us both safely to the top and down again, if not this trip then at some future date. He was wedded to that landscape; his family had lived in the valley for five hundred years. He would surely be there the next time I visited.

In the end, a combination of pending obligations and insufficient courage drew me away from rather than up the mountain, but I returned to the village three more times during the next decade, held in thrall by the mesmerizing peak, hiking always to the climbers' hut perched upon the northwest ridge to stare upward at the fearsome rock, trying to calculate the physical effort required to climb a vertical mile attached to life by little more than a nylon rope and a steel bolt. Where did one find the courage for such an undertaking, standing with nothing between a meager toe hold and the rock-strewn glacier below but six thousand feet of gripless air? No, it no longer seemed possible, not in my life. I was growing older, my cautious nature proving increasingly resistant to the risk, the contemplation alone leaving me breathless. Ultimately, a failure of the imagination kept me earthbound: I simply could not envision myself pinioned to a vertical rock face halfway to the troposphere. The cemetery below the church contained the remains of all too many who had misstepped, including twenty of the village's own skilled guides. And yet, so long as Rony continued to rope himself to the mountain, the possibility remained that I might just accept his offer. I wasn't getting any younger, but men in midlife are known to take all manner of risk, some foolish, some transformative.

But the news of Rony's death put an end to that thought. What had lurked for so long at the fringes of possibility returned to the realm of the unattainable. Even men born to scramble up and down those treacherous walls—Rony had once climbed to the summit twice in a single day—were occasionally overcome by them. And when they fell they left behind widows and children and a sense of unnecessary loss. Was the pursuit worth the life? Perhaps to Rony, but not to me. That simple equation divided the mountaineer from the bystander. Only those willing to accept the terrible calculus of death and desire scaled those heights. I sent my condolences to his widow and received a reply steeped in the resignation and emotional restraint that a mountain guide's wife must learn to cultivate. Rony had died doing what he loved. She had been blessed to have him more years than she had ever dared to hope.

I arrived in Zermatt last summer hoping to learn more about the circumstances of Rony's fatal fall. At the church where his widow had played organ during Sunday services throughout her married life, I was told she had retired from her post and now spent summers abroad. In the adjacent cemetery I found several graves decorated with decaying climbing ropes and others bearing Rony's surname, though not his. But at the mountaineering office, a young guide told me exactly where

Rony was buried and what little was known of his last moments on the mountain.

They had found his body and that of his client at the base of the sheer east face. The evidence of rope and crampons, boots and ax, suggested that they had just come off the summit and successfully crossed the topmost ice field, pausing to remove their spikes in preparation for the long, rocky descent. But something had gone fatally wrong: a sudden, powerful gust of wind, falling rock or ice, a misstep, a simple lapse of judgment, or perhaps a heart attack. In the end, the young guide said with the cold-eyed concession of his trade, they would never really know.

My last evening I returned to the cemetery and found Rony's geranium-covered grave amid those of his ancestors. I stood a moment remembering his weather-beaten face and halting English, his subtle, self-deprecating humor, his love of that incomparable landscape, and his quiet courage. Roped together, we might have climbed above the clouds. But the opportunity had passed; I was beyond such dreams now and so was he. By the cemetery entrance stood a memorial to the local guides who had died in mountaineering accidents since 1890. On the granite monument, etched with a climber's hands reaching to a high cliff, were inscribed the words: "Here we lost our life; there we found it again on the sacred mountain of the Lord." A plaque bearing Rony's name and the date of his death had been recently added. He was sixty-nine.

SINGING TO THE DEAD

Maybe no one would come, I thought, looking out at the empty sanctuary on the eve of September 11. Ninety of us, representing eleven local choruses, planned to mark the first anniversary of the terrorist attack by singing the Mozart *Requiem* at 8:46 the following morning—the moment the first terror-piloted plane struck the north tower of the World Trade Center—joining hundreds of choruses around the world in global commemoration of the nearly 3,000 victims who died that terrible day in Manhattan, Washington, and Shanksville. "This will be our reply to violence," Leonard Bernstein famously remarked in another context, "to make music more intensely, more beautifully, more devotedly than ever before." But would anyone be listening? In the welter of memorial activities planned for the anniversary, from the laying of wreaths to the reading of names, from morning prayer services to candlelight vigils, who would find time to stop for an hour to listen to a chance assembly of amateur and professional singers performing Mozart's masterwork in a small suburban church?

Then again, for whom were we singing this requiem mass, anyway? We had come together to memorialize the dead and provide comfort for ourselves and the community. Crowded together on makeshift risers, we could think of no more fitting way to mark the day than through music. And perhaps it would be just as fitting to sing to a vacant chapel, performing for the victims alone. In life those 3,000 souls would never have fit into the small sanctuary; in death they might all hover just above our heads, deriving whatever solace they might from the knowledge that they are not forgotten, that they are mourned not only by their families, but by an entire nation.

Had I taken a moment to consider the death toll in our county alone, read the local newspaper that afternoon, visited any of the websites devoted to this worldwide "Rolling Requiem," or spent a moment in the church office manning the phones, I would have realized that more than memory would fill those pews. And when I arrived shortly before eight the next morning, the sanctuary was already beginning to fill with a silent stream of mourners. In the rehearsal room behind the alter each singer was given a badge bearing the name of one of the hundred or so local victims, mine prompting the ironic thought: where but in America could one find a Jew singing a requiem mass in a Presbyterian church for a Jewish victim of Islamic extremists? Was it that very plurality, that vibrant intermingling of cultures, that our enemies found so threatening? Or had some fevered, abstract hate so stripped them of basic human compassion that any death, even the death of children, seemed not only warranted but honorable?

At 8:44 we filed wordlessly into the sun-filled sanctuary, instantly realizing this would not be a requiem mass sung only to the dead. The pews were packed, additional seats lined the aisles, people stood three and four deep beside the windows, crowded the stairs, the balcony, the foyer. "This is going to be difficult," the conductor had warned us in the choir room. "There will be powerful distractions of heart and mind. Try to remain focused." And just before he raised his baton, I noticed a woman seated directly behind him, her face a mask of grief. My own eyes began to tear, my throat to close, but the sudden emergence of music wrested my attention from mourning and plunged me into the center of the sound, buoyed by the resonant voices around me. Until the final notes died away I kept my eyes fixed upon the conductor. Only then, in the reverent silence that followed, did I return my gaze to the grieving woman, her hand still over her mouth, her eyes awash in tears, as though the memory of loss were as devastating now as it had been a year ago.

Slowly, quietly, the audience dispersed, many lingering in the church dooryard, unwilling to relinquish the mood of remembrance, the atmosphere of grace. A handful clung to the pews, including that still-stunned widow, surrounded now by friends and relatives. What comfort could she take from the knowledge that so many others suffered as she did, others in that very room? What was it like for the widows of great conflicts to visit the battlefields where loved ones fell, knowing that every mourning visitor, every hapless victim shared a similar fate? Did flags, color guards, posthumous medals, memorial speeches, or music ease their pain?

Before leaving the church I climbed to the balcony and looked down upon the now empty altar, the risers gone, the lecterns and tables restored, the lights dimmed, the sanctuary doors closed. The young widow remained, alone now, privately facing the abyss of her grief. For the rest of us it was time to move on; we had performed our sacred task. But how and when would she move on? What solace could an hour of song truly provide?

Turning from that place, I thought of Emily Dickinson's musing on death:

> *This is the Hour of Lead—*
> *Remembered, if outlived,*
> *As Freezing persons, recollect the Snow—*
> *First—Chill—then Stupor—then the letting go—*

There would be no "letting go," not now, not yet, perhaps not ever. The love of those lost would continue to flame, to sear, to ache and nothing the world did to acknowledge the private agony, the public loss, would diminish it. Music might act as temporary anodyne, but the gnawing emptiness would inevitably return, perhaps even more acute than before. We could be forgiven for not holding the dead in our hearts every waking moment, but the mourners knew no such relief.

I climbed over the hill toward home, pausing near the top to look back at the church, it's outer doors now closed. Through the trees came the sound of a commuter train rumbling toward the city. Overhead a nearly inaudible jet etched a thin white line across the canvas blue sky, heading west, toward another time zone, another commemoration of loss as 8:46 circled the globe, rotating with memory and grief.

ON THE HOME FRONT

"Is Gary still stateside?" I asked his parents as we sat down to dinner. The very use of the term, "stateside," seemed to conjure images of war. Their son was a Navy SEAL, one of the military's special operations forces, trained in unconventional warfare. In recent years the SEALs had seen service combating international terrorism and drug trafficking. Gary's own involvement in these operations remained classified. He never spoke of his postings and his parents knew not to ask. In truth, they preferred not to know, content to take their son at his word when he told them he would be away for six weeks on a "training exercise." The alternative was too unsettling. They spent more time than ever in prayer, they told us, and lost no opportunity to visit their son between postings.

"He's awaiting his redeployment orders," John replied, slipping on reading glasses to glance at the menu. I studied his face, searching for signs of worry, finding instead an odd detachment, a seeming indifference to the darkening clouds shadowing us all. But I knew better, knew his every second thought concerned the safety of his only son. "Probably ship out any day now," he added without looking up.

"Not necessarily," Martha countered, a hint of annoyance in her usually docile voice. They'd been over this ground often, I suspected, her husband assuming a fatalistic tone—what would be would be; the military was a dangerous occupation, after all—while she clung to the belief that her baby, her boy, would somehow avoid the very risks he was trained to confront. Hadn't he already survived more than six years in the elite corps. Why shouldn't he continue to be blessed with good fortune? Four more years and he would retire from the military. Maybe then she'd be able to sleep soundly again.

"Will he be shipped to the Persian Gulf?" I asked.

"He certainly hopes so," John replied.

"Not necessarily," Martha countered.

"He can't wait to go," John insisted, mistaking his wife's response. "It's what he's been preparing to do for years."

"I meant he won't necessarily be shipped to the Gulf," she corrected. "He's a medic. They can use his skills anywhere."

"Anywhere people get hurt," John murmured sardonically, returning his eyes to the menu.

"What's good here?" my wife asked, trying to pilot the conversation toward calmer waters. I should have been more sensitive to the tensions my questions provoked. I saw the worry in Martha's eyes the moment we sat down. She had the weary, heavy-lidded look we all wore back when our children were infants and we stayed up nights nursing them through illness. But I couldn't help wondering how the parents of active-duty soldiers coped with the knowledge that at any moment their children might be going to war.

Each morning I opened the newspaper with a vague dread, fearing the banner headline that would announce the opening salvo of another war against Iraq, shuddered whenever a news bulletin flashed across the TV screen, remembering the first late-night reports from Baghdad in 1991. Like any child of the sixties, I dreaded the prospect of a protracted war consuming tens of thousands of our young men, my son among them. He was only sixteen now, but what protection did a two-year deferment provide back in 1965? I saw his face superimposed upon the thousands of soldiers pictured daily in the media, men and women and the tons of matériel needed to support them loading up and shipping out, more than a quarter of a million soldiers amassing on the Iraqi border.

I wondered, too, what it must be like to live within those borders, protected by little more than the self-restraint of the most powerful army in the world. Despite our insistence that we seek only "regime change," not war with the Iraqi people, the certainty of "collateral damage" must render such claims of little comfort. Ours is a fearsome might, an awesome responsibility.

We ordered dinner, our eyes occasionally drifting to the TV set over the bar, relieved each time the image presented nothing more ominous than the latest sports highlights. Conversation drifted to peacetime concerns: how their daughter was enjoying her new job, how ours was adjusting to college, recent movies, summer plans. But that brought us back around to the war. How could anyone make long-range travel plans with the prospect of war looming?

"Why can't we just keep the pressure on, like we've been doing the last few months?" my wife wondered aloud. "We don't need to go to war so long as Iraq cooperates with the inspectors."

"I've never seen the United Nations so effective," Martha added. For the first time in recent memory, it seemed to have teeth. The inspectors were getting results; Iraq was allowing access to weapons sites, destroying missiles.

"But Saddam's an evil man," John declared reluctantly. "He's killed thousands of his own people and wouldn't think twice about using a nuclear bomb on Israel, if he had one. We can't allow that kind of madness to terrorize the world."

Few would lament the overthrow of so violent a man, but what about the law of unintended consequences, the rise to power of factions more violently unpredictable than the current regime, the incubation of Al Quaeda-like fanaticism within a whole new generation?

"Is Saddam's removal worth one American life?" I asked, thinking of his son.

"We lost 3,000 innocent American lives pretending the world couldn't harm us," John insisted. "We have to stop evil in its tracks, wherever it lurks. There are a lot of people out there who hate us and wish us ill."

Can we go to war against them all, I wondered, but asked instead, "How does Gary feel about all this?"

"That the world is a dangerous place and complacency only makes it more so," John replied. "If it has to be his life that is sacrificed to make the world a little safer, I believe he's ready and willing to pay that price."

I wasn't going to ask my next question, but I didn't have to. John looked across the table at Martha, his own eyes suddenly as vulnerable as hers, and said, "I don't know if I could face life without him." It seemed the first time he had openly admitted that devastating vulnerability to himself or his wife.

Martha took his hand. "We won't have to," she insisted, her face suddenly as resolute as his was unsure. "He's going to be fine. He's still here."

I looked away, realizing how shadowed their lives had become by dread, how many countless parents, spouses, and children now sat glued to the news, their happiness hanging in the balance. My eyes returned to the TV by the bar: spring training in the Florida sun. Life on the home front was continuing as though nothing were amiss. Soon the last of the winter snow would melt, the trees would begin to blossom, and perhaps, just perhaps, reason and restraint would prevail, violence would be staid, the mandate of the United Nations would be fulfilled, a new, free Iraq would emerge from the tortured sands of the old, and the men and women and machines would return home safe and sound, their mission accomplished without a shot fired.

THE PHONY WAR

In the fall of 1939 she had fled to a remote farm in Normandy, fearing an aerial bombardment of Paris. Two days earlier Hitler had invaded Poland; France and Britain had declared war. For three uncertain weeks she listened to news of the Polish collapse and of the mobilization of Allied forces, expecting war to erupt across Europe. But by the first of October an eerie calm had settled over the continent. Warsaw had been occupied, all of Poland subdued; the French had sent fresh troops to reinforce the Maginot line; Great Britain had prepared an amphibious invasion force; but the feared western offensive had not materialized and perhaps never would. So she and thousands of others returned to Paris and prayed for lasting peace.

And for the next six months peace seemed possible. Though children carried gas masks to school and mothers knitted socks for soldiers at the front, the prospect of war receded. The daily papers ran cartoons of fraternizing French and German troops doing little but their laundry and waving to each other across the demilitarized zone. Yes, there were ominous rumblings in the east: the Soviet Union had attacked Finland; but that was a distant and different war, Stalin's not Hitler's. Through the winter and early spring of 1940 it began to seem as though the declared and dreaded war against Germany might never come, that Hitler might content himself with his conquests in eastern Europe. And she breathed easier for it.

But others were growing tired of this "Phony War," this empty Allied declaration lacking teeth. With millions of men mobilized, what were they waiting for? It was time to put a stop to Hitler's aggression and quickly, while his troops were still recovering from their Polish campaign. How much more territory was he to be allowed to annex? In three years he had reoccupied the Rhineland, marched unopposed into Austria, annexed Czechoslovakia, conquered Poland. Now Stalin was subduing Finland, and Norway's ports were under siege. And still, the Allies waited.

Those old enough to recall the carnage of the First World War were less eager to return to the battlefield, remembering the years locked in deadly trench warfare, the tens of millions of casualties, the ultimate futility of it all. Had that war been staid, a whole generation might have been spared. Given more time, diplomacy might have eased the tensions, resolved the conflicts, muzzled the madmen and their war machines. War was not inevitable; patience was critical, peace must be given every opportunity to take root. Let this Phony War, this uneasy truce, persist, they argued, until saner minds prevailed.

The same thought returned to her more than sixty years later as she watched the nightly news reports from Kuwait through yet another tense winter and early spring. This time it was not Hitler but Hussein, not the Allies but America, largely alone, and this time the outcome seemed preordained. Still, that gnawing dread, that remembered fear of unleashed forces unsettled her. Why rush to battle if weapons inspectors were making headway? Why abandon all diplomatic efforts when the UN seemed to be exacting crucial concessions? Why expose our soldiers, our sons and daughters, to hostilities without provocation? Sixty years ago a madman had been loosed upon the land, wreaking havoc wherever he turned, murdering millions. Appeasement had only whetted his appetite for further concessions. But that was not the case now. Iraq had been cordoned and confined, monitored, patrolled, threatened with devastating attack. Surely, with the genie so tightly stoppered, diplomacy could be allowed more time to accomplish its ends, the UN's carrot reinforced by America's stick.

But the weight of time seemed to militate against peace, each day drawing the nation nearer to battle. A course had been charted, men and machines set in motion, great sums of money expended, personal honor and national pride invoked. The generals were eager to wage war, the soldiers to fight, the media to report each battle and bomb blast. The sheer momentum of a quarter of a million men could be felt half a world away. The troops likened themselves to football players in three-point stance, adrenaline pumping, eyes narrowed, awaiting the snap, the lurch forward, the crush of bodies. They were both apprehensive and eager to discover what they were made of, how well they would stand up to this ultimate test. The anticipation felt like a hunger, they said, a dull ache, a desire. They were too young to appreciate the consequences of that craving, its morbid aftertaste, she thought. God willing they never would.

So many greater provocations had passed with little or inadequate response in recent years: the mass murder of millions in Africa, in Cambodia, in the Balkans. Why was the line being drawn here, in this sand? Why had the nation allowed so vast a store of its precious resources to be committed to this campaign? What really was at stake in Iraq? Sixty years ago the choice had seemed so clear—Hitler's motiveless malignity, the pandemic terror of the rapacious Nazi state versus democracy and freedom. Were the consequences of inaction as dire today? She didn't think so. And this time we were far from inactive; extraordinary pressure was being brought to bear; an aggressive policy of containment was in place. The grim prognostications of the president and his advisors seemed overblown. If weapons of mass destruction in volatile hands were truly our greatest concern, Korea seemed far more deserving of our attention, so too India and Pakistan.

Each night she went to bed grateful for another day of peace, hoping the morning headlines would not bring an end to this "phony war." Though there was so much less at risk for her personally—she would not have to flee her home; her children were not in uniform—the war threatened her understanding of American values. Her adopted land was not a nation that initiated conflict, but rather came to the rescue of others, herself included. This impending war threatened to set a dangerous precedent, one the congress of nations was already mindful of:

the lone superpower exerting its will unilaterally, heedless of world opinion.

The coming war might prove phony in ways those early months of World War II never were: the death and destruction would be real enough, but the rationale might prove wholly counterfeit. The unintended consequences of our involvement might ultimately cause us far greater ill. One had only to consider previous U.S. efforts at "regime change"—in Iran, Cuba, Chile, Vietnam, Guatemala, Russian-occupied Afghanistan, and in Iraq itself forty years earlier—to have serious doubts about the wisdom of such intervention.

The massed troops would not stand down, pack up, and return home without a fight, she realized. A critical juncture had passed, a deadly momentum achieved. There seemed no stopping this war now. And perhaps she would come to applaud the consequences. But history would be the final judge, and that history would be written and rewritten as the endless tide of action and reaction shed new light and rendered new judgment on what we did as a nation in the days to come.

THE FATE OF OUR MOST CHERISHED WORDS

The books begin arriving in early spring, left in cardboard boxes and shopping bags or neatly piled in stacks by the back door like so many bricks. Some mornings a wild disorder prevails, as though the volumes quarreled during the night, had "words," then fell to blows, lying now in mute disarray, the arriving librarians stepping gingerly around and through the thicket blocking the entrance. Other mornings a single homeless orphan stands neatly pressed and submissive just off the path, meekly seeking a new home.

Where do they come from, these thousands of unwanted books? What homes once took them in and have now abandoned them? Who so patiently underlined the text or received them inscribed from friends only now to give them away? What stories of love and loss do they evoke, apart from the tales their pages plainly tell? In most instances there can be no knowing. The donors remain largely anonymous, dropping off books after hours or unceremoniously during the day, grateful, it seems, to be rid of what once provided so many hours of comfort, knowledge, or simple diversion.

In more than one instance, death seems to have prompted the separation. How else explain the letting go of treasures, leather-bound books once oiled and dusted, inscribed with best wishes from friends and relatives for holidays and birthdays, on the occasion of graduations and confirmations, of babies born and children married, upon accession to great heights, in consolation for deep loss, as the caprice of friendship, the expression of abiding love, in gratitude or supplication, or merely in jest.

Entire lives seem refracted through these donations: the wooden wine crate packed to bursting with nothing but English poets, the three-dozen librettos from the Metropolitan Opera, the complete mysteries of Agatha Christie, the two yards of books on bread baking, gardening, photography, Asian brush painting, the history of western civilization.

In some shopping bags nothing but changing fashion prevails: the must-read volumes of seasons past, the best sellers, diet books, how-to-talk-with-your-teen handbooks, cookbooks, exercise books, the latest in travel guides, in Wall Street scandal, in self-satisfied politicians, business tycoons, and TV personalities trumpeting the secrets of their success, of their sex lives, of their waistlines.

The inevitable passage of time is played out in the donation of high school study guides, Cliff Notes, SAT prep manuals. Every paperback title ever assigned high school students arrives in multiple copies—*The Great Gatsby, Hamlet, The Catcher in the Rye, The Sound and the Fury, Ethan Frome*—the covers bent, torn and deeply etched with ballpoint tattoos, the pages dog-eared, margins marred with doodles, phone numbers, occasional bursts of insight, a teacher's observation.

One might learn volumes about a town's inner life from the books left at the library door: the issues of self-image and self-improvement that preoccupy, the dreams that motivate, the hobbies that divert. One glimpses a community's sense of personal and political history, its small comforts and intellectual strivings, its pretensions and passions, and the ways it fills its quiet moments when nothing else beckons but a book.

One learns, too, about the many ways we mark the place we left off reading, and one learns about forgetfulness. Did a phone call tear the reader away so abruptly that the only bookmark at hand was the Con Edison bill lying on the desk, or the check just written to the PTA, or the humorous birthday card that arrived that afternoon? And why was the book never finished, the check, the bill, the card never retrieved? In the basement where the books are sorted and priced, a box slowly fills with the ephemera that fall from these many pages: yellow newspaper clippings, handwritten letters, finely tooled leather bookmarks, small silver and gold page clips, laminated memorial prayer cards. How much time was spent searching for the missing bill, the lost check, the cherished letter? What misunderstandings ensued, whose feelings were hurt?

And what about all those loving inscriptions? Did they give the donors pause as they pulled the books from their shelves and decided it was time to part company? Did they flip through the pages one last time or simply proceed with cold-eyed determination to get the job done? And if they paused to read, "To My Dearest Friend, from one who thinks these same thoughts but could never express them half so well, Yours always," did they reconsider a moment before deciding to go ahead with it, to lighten up and let go of the past? Or had that friendship, like so much else in life, long since withered, leaving not fond memory but bitterness and regret?

And so, over a long weekend and into the next week, the community room hums with the fevered browsings of ardent book buyers, many of them, by their own admission, responsible for the donations they now rifle, twenty thousand books arrayed spine up on fifty tables and in open boxes on the floor, on library shelving carts, across a grand piano, lining steps to a small stage.

"You read that already," one browser tells another, both toting overloaded book bags. "I always end up buying back the books I donated," the first replies, laughing. "I don't have room for these," another tells the cashier, "or time to read them all." A third murmurs, "My husband is going to kill me. We just gave away this many." A father tells his young daughter, "I read that when I was your age. You're going to love it!"

The days pass and the same question begins to surface as the dwindling crowd surveys the still congested tables: what is to become of all these leftovers? Nearly half the donations remain, all in good condition. The village has reached its saturation point. It can't absorb another book. If only a home could be found for those that remain, a hospital, a school, a church rummage sale, a second-hand book store, a homeless shelter, the Salvation Army. They have all been tried. No one needs used books anymore. "If only there were a small town somewhere looking to start its own library?" a patron suggests. "This could seed their collection." But if there is such a town, no one knows where.

The sale ends, a few charitable organizations arrive and fill their trunks, but the tables remain full. Some books return to the basement to reemerge at next year's sale, others shift to tables by the library door, part of a small perpetual book sale. But most simply end up, as most books ultimately do, consigned to landfill. No lover of books can hear that with indifference. Though we might give our precious books away, we do so in the belief that they will live on after us as literature always has, among grateful, enlightened readers. But books, like mankind, are mortal. The species may endure but individuals return to earth; so too even our most cherished words.

ART AND ALCHEMY

"The gods are definitely against us!" a woman in a makeshift hat of plastic wrap moaned as the rain worsened. We had just ducked inside her booth at the annual outdoor art show, moving slowly from one canvas-roofed stall to the next, lingering among the oil and watercolor paintings, photographs, and aquatint prints, occasionally pretending more interest than we felt when the rain grew heavier, trapping us briefly as it curtained each cubicle with long, crystal beads of runoff. None of the booths were truly watertight, forcing the artists to jury-rig additional tarps and plastic sheets in a desperate effort to preserve their work and keep their would-be patrons dry. It was not the kind of weekend they had envisioned; even the most seasoned road show veterans were disheartened.

The weather, and these ad hoc efforts to cope with it, seemed emblematic of their lives as artists: never mind an indifferent public, nature itself conspired against their every effort to gain a measure of recognition and a modest self-sufficiency. No sooner had they set up shop, many traveling several hundred miles for the privilege of exhibiting and selling their work a few miles north of Manhattan, than the tail end of a late-September hurricane turned the sky leaden and thinned the usual flood of prospective patrons to a mere trickle, leaving the artists despondent. They had labored long and hard over their works and paid dearly for their booths, hoping to recoup their expenses and perhaps even earn enough to support their habit for another year; but with so few people braving the storm and fewer still willing to carry precious artwork home in the rain, their prospects dimmed. By late Sunday afternoon many had abandoned their booths for the cold comforts of the cook tent, drowning their disappointment in hot cider, apple pie, and pretzels, a few quietly declaring that this was it, their last show. Come Monday they would begin looking for a real job. Art just didn't pay.

One woman had driven six hours from Northern Vermont to sell her intaglio prints of stone walls and wild mushrooms, and was spending as much for her weekend motel room as she normally budgeted for a month's groceries. By mid-Sunday she had abandoned all hope of recovering her travel expenses, but was still counting on a few small sales to fund her trip home. A man from Pittsburgh who carved exquisitely detailed decoys said if he had to live on his earnings rather than his pension, he and his wife would have long since boiled and eaten his wooden ducks.

Clinging to steaming coffee cups, my wife and I ambled from tent to tent, finding that the combination of pattering rain, unpeopled booths, and muted light enhanced the work, evoking the rare vibrancy that rain-wet autumn leaves possess, as well as a feeling of isolation akin to the conditions under which much of the work was produced. The artist remains a highly romantic figure in the American imagination, envied for his rebelliousness and vision, his resourceful solitude, his ability to ignore the grinding poverty of city garret or mountain cabin in the single-minded pursuit of the evanescent. The necessary condition of creativity, many believe, is an eremitic seclusion that forces the artist to confront his own demons, forging out of personal struggle a universal truth.

That truth was what we sought as we moved from tent to tent, hoping to be drawn in suddenly by a painting's interpretive power, a photograph's penetrating clarity, a sculpture's human warmth, by the artist's ability to reveal the eternal in the ephemeral. I wanted to stand mute and overwhelmed, confronting the commonplace with new eyes, new appreciation, with a renewed sense of wonder and awe, to discover the sublime in something as pedestrian and familiar as a human hand, a withered leaf, a heap of yarn. And here and there, in shadowy corners, we discovered it. But perhaps too late.

Overhearing the artists' dispirited conversations, I knew how little it would take to restore their confidence: a few kind words, an occasional sale. Some needed nothing more than a companion's enduring faith. Artists have always possessed the alchemical ability to survive on little more than hope. For a society preoccupied with the steadily escalating costs of basic necessities, there is no greater bargain than the artist. To them we owe our ability to see beyond the temporal surface of things. The artist is responsible for enlarging the field of human thought and emotion, of augmenting the beautiful, of engendering joy. After seeing a Rembrandt portrait, a Monet haystack, or a Michelangelo sculpture, can we ever look upon the world in the same way again? Our perception is forever altered: we see through new eyes. What a lifetime of change, of loss, of regret eventually evokes in us all, the artist can effect instantly, enriching the present moment rather than simply eulogizing the past.

We had come in search of such vision, hoping to bring home an emblem of it, something that would remind us of the infinite potential for beauty locked in the very weeds under our feet. And in several booths we encountered the new amid the seemingly familiar, among vegetables and fieldstones, waves and wild horses, a child's tear-streaked face and a pealing clapboard facade, all astonishing in their unexpected beauty. And because these were not world-famous artists with world-class expectations, we could acquire the evidence of sublimity for little more than the cost of a new pair of shoes. How much farther we could travel in such company. So we wrote a few checks and with each small purchase felt as though a judgment of failure had been staid, that this invaluable enterprise would endure yet another day to enrich not simply the artist but us all. Ours was not the act of patronage but admiration, not a gesture of appropriation but gratitude. In those few damp hours we encountered art's great consequence—a new way of seeing and feeling and thinking. It was worth a thousand times what we paid.

IN LOVE WITH SHAKESPEARE

Raised on Racine, my mother could be forgiven the confusion that prompted her to take my six-year-old brother to see *Tom Jones* under the mistaken impression that they were about to watch a Mississippi idyll full of fence painting and river rafting. When the other adults in line cast reproving glances her way it began to dawn on her that something was amiss. Where were all the children, she wondered? Once inside it didn't take her long to realize that she had stumbled into a tale of English debauchery and beat a hasty retreat, my little brother glancing back over his shoulder and asking in a too-loud voice why everyone on the screen was eating with their fingers.

I could not admit to the same misunderstanding as I chaperoned my twelve- and fourteen-year-old daughters into *Shakespeare in Love*. For one, the movie bore an "R" rating, for another, I had already seen it. Yes, there was a little nudity, I admitted to my shocked mother (still not over her gaff after thirty-six years), but it was tastefully presented as the impassioned embraces of young Will Shakespeare and his beautiful muse, Viola de Lesseps, a couple as haplessly devoted to each other as Romeo and Juliet and just as intoxicated by words. I wanted my children to discover that such a relationship not only to another but to language was possible, that poetry not only gave voice to such passion, making it manifest and rendering it accessible to the world, but preserved, even elevated it. And I wanted them to know there was more to life and art than the likes of *Dumb and Dumber*, *Seinfeld*, and *Friends*. How could they be expected to strive for something more exalted in their own lives if their only models (parents aside) were so shallow?

Because the movie was Shakespeare—well, pseudo-Shakespeare—I was willing to overlook the "R" rating in the hope that my daughters would come to associate the Bard not with things antiquated and incomprehensible but passionate and pertinent. So great, in fact, was my desire to introduce them to Shakespeare's romantic vision that my wife and I conveniently forgot about Rosaline.

But two minutes into the film we turned to each other and muttered an embarrassed, "Uh, oh!" as the strumpet appeared on screen in the first of two highly compromising positions. Instantly I realized I had fallen victim to my own adolescence. Thirty-two years earlier, at the impressionable age of fifteen, I had seen a preview for the Franco Zeffirelli film *Romeo and Juliet* and had fallen instantly in love with the image of myself and the girl sitting beside me as star-crossed lovers. I was captivated by the totality of a passion surpassing all claims of fealty, family, friends, and reason. What could be more appealing to a befuddled teenager overwhelmed by pubescent impulses and the looming responsibilities of incipient maturity than the possibility of escape to an isle of eros with no other care than to embrace a beautiful young woman in the heat of a Verona summer? I couldn't wait to see the film.

Unfortunately, by the time it was released, my Juliet had become a Rosaline, relinquishing me for someone older and more experienced. I watched the movie in the company of another, a girl who, even under the narcotic influence of the moment, could not transport me to that realm of romantic consummation I had dreamt of for months. I had been left more than "unsatisfied," I had been left thoroughly disillusioned. I might enjoy the film but not the prospect of incarnating it. Mine was not to be a life of all-consuming passion; I was not to be secretly betrothed to a beautiful Juliet, committed from an early age and for life, freed from the punishing vicissitudes of adolescent longings and betrayals. I was not to know a love strong enough to endure banishment, brave enough to embrace death. I was to be a frustrated, pimple-faced fifteen year old, struggling unaccompanied through the baffling uncertainties of tenth grade.

For months I pined. And then, miraculously, I met my Juliet and fell hopelessly and irrevocably in love. Within weeks I told my parents I intended to marry the girl, and one summer night summoned her to her bedroom window with a shower of pebbles then climbed a trellis to the second story and into her arms. We attended college together where a gifted teacher took us beyond *Romeo and Juliet* to an appreciation of all thirty-seven of Shakespeare's plays. Following graduation we married. Now, thirty years later, I wanted to introduce our daughters to the playwright in the foolish hope that the sense of passionate commitment embodied in his work might step off the screen and into their lives.

But our children seem to inhabit a world indifferent to, if not completely devoid of, the romantic impulse that united us, a love that is both an enlargement and a negation of the self, that begins by imitating art and ends in absorbing that art into life, making it flesh. Their music celebrates anger, alienation, and violence; their movies ugliness, stupidity, and greed; their books, well, they don't have any books. Do I sound like my own father condemning the callow culture of the sixties? Absolutely. Isn't that what it means to grow up, to bear children, to accumulate regrets? My parents hoped opera would humanize their rock-n-roll corrupted children, I resorted to Shakespeare. Both proved miserably inadequate. Each generation finds its own talisman, its own touchstone.

As the final credits rolled, I emerged into the light transported anew by the romance, delighted by the comedy, enchanted by the cleverness. My daughters appeared unmoved. Wiping tears from my eyes, I asked how they liked the film. They shrugged. Wasn't Viola beautiful? I probed. She was okay, they responded. And young Will Shakespeare? Not their type. How about the play within the play, *Romeo and Juliet*? Too old-fashioned. Was there anything they had liked? The popcorn, my younger daughter declared. Yeah, and the coming attractions, the older one added. As for the nudity, no big deal, they assured me with worldly hauteur.

Like most obsessions, mine with Shakespeare has, thus far, proved nontransferable. Nevertheless, I recently borrowed the old Zeffirelli movie from our local library and asked my daughters to watch it with me. The younger one expressed interest but said she had a date with *Ally McBeal*. The older one shook her head: she'd read the play in school; Shakespeare was boring. So my wife and I watched the movie alone, holding hands, two superannuated romantics reliving a time of great passion, the flame that had once annealed us transmuted after three decades from pyrotechnic flourish to the steady glow of abiding love and comfortable companionability. Romeo and Juliet, by definition, cannot survive more than a single night of incendiary passion. Knowledge, whether acquired in the Garden of Eden or behind Verona's orchard walls, inevitably leads to transformation. But to have known such love, to have felt such exulted communion, is to have touched heaven. Shakespeare led us there. And we'll never forget it.

NOT JUST ANY PROM

Thirty-two years ago my future wife and I approached a small card table stationed just outside the high school cafeteria and purchased two prom tickets. Sales had been less than brisk up to that point. We were only the fourth couple out of a senior class of some 450 students to buy the $25 ticket for two. Two weeks later, after only a handful of tickets had been sold, the prom was cancelled and our money refunded. So far as I know, it was the only year in our high school's history without a prom. The war in Vietnam was generally held accountable for this lack of school spirit: we were all too busy picketing draft boards and marching on Washington to bother with gowns and corsages.

Thankfully, times have changed, and recent cataclysmic events have cemented rather than fractured this year's graduating seniors. As the big night approaches, prom fever is running high, preoccupying our daughter and all her friends. Having missed our own, my wife and I are taking vicarious pleasure in the preparations and excitement. But the cost has us reeling. More than simple inflation seems to account for the difference. Today's prom does not share the same universe as those of our era. Its order of magnitude is altogether different; it's a 747 to the canvas-winged bi-planes of an earlier age.

So, what does it cost? You don't want to know. The prom ticket alone is now $280 per couple, more than eleven times what we paid in the spring of 1970. Of course, we expected little more than a brightly decorated gymnasium, soda and chips, and a slightly more upscale band than the teenage groups that usually played school dances. Our daughter has far greater expectations. Her class will not gather in a gym or cafeteria but in Manhattan at Chelsea Piers. They will not arrive there on foot or by car but by stretch limo, paying as much as $300 a couple for the privilege. When the prom ends, they will move en masse to a club across town that charges an additional $80 a couple before their limos whisk them back home for the $30 traditional pool breakfast.

Is anyone doing the math? So far I'm up to roughly $700 per couple and that doesn't include prom gowns and fittings, dyed shoes and handbags, tuxedos, after-prom "club dresses," jewelry, hair styling, makeup, nail appointments, corsages, and boutonnieres. In a single generation, the high school prom has gone from being a $25 teen dance to a celebrity wedding, costing, what a friend of ours refers to as a "suburban unit." (Virtually every expense in suburban life, he maintains, can be calculated in thousand-dollar increments or units: orthodontia, five units; bathroom renovation, 25 units; car repair, half a unit to two units.) It's madness!

Who is paying for all this extravagance, I wonder? I know I am. But is every other senior parent blithely doing the same, or are some enterprising, self-sufficient seniors taking it upon themselves to foot this lavish indulgence? (Did someone just whisper, "Get real!") I only ask because I was never consulted, never polled, never so much as warned, simply presented with the bill. If memory serves, we once fought a revolution over a similar oversight. On this occasion, however, I kept my troops quartered and only ranted and fumed a bit. "Is the limo really necessary?" I asked our graduating senior. "You're all going to the same place, why not hire a bus? And why does it have to be in Manhattan? What's wrong with using the high school or a local hotel? And what's with this club business? Isn't one extravagant party per night sufficient? And a club dress? What's the point of paying so much for a prom gown if you're not even going to wear it the whole night? And since when can't you do you own hair, nails and makeup? Isn't this all completely out of proportion and totally out of control?" To which our daughter answered: "Dad, it's my senior prom." End of discussion.

So, naturally, we paid every bill and applauded each gown brought home on contingency, each club dress, the shorts and T-shirts intended for the pool breakfast, the jewelry loaned and gifted by mother and grandmother; we made appointments for fittings, negotiated with limo companies, spent days in search of matching shoes and handbags, and we signed up to scramble eggs at 3:00 a.m. by the pool.

Do I object to all of this? Of course I do. Am I complicitous? Of course I am. Should something be done to reign in this excess? Absolutely, and soon. In two years we face twice the expense when our twins graduate. So who's going to do something? I haven't a clue. I'm the very model of ambivalence. If this were my prom, the prom I never attended, I'd want my last memory of high school to be situated in the place that meant so much to me for four years, not some faceless catering hall or nightclub. Does my daughter share this sentiment? Not for a minute. And if I spent so much on a prom gown or, in my case, a tuxedo, I wouldn't be in such a hurry to change out of it. But there too I'm hopelessly out of date. A single change of clothes is no longer adequate for a night on the town. And all those fashion assistants called in on the day of the big event are equally essential, I've come to understand. Hollywood has set the tone. Every lavish party has become a premiere. Life is now in constant competition with a parallel celluloid universe that sets our standards of behavior and conditions our expectations and responses. Perhaps, somewhere, lurking behind all this excessive preparation, is the understanding that what truly awaits our seniors is not stardom but simply dinner and dancing. And perhaps that's just too prosaic a realization. Why not inflate the whole event, extending its five-hour duration by several weeks of busy, breathless anticipation? Why not transform a mere prom into a royal wedding or better yet, the Academy Awards.

So what's my point? I guess I'm just checking in, comparing notes, giving voice to middle-aged astonishment. Truth be told, I'm looking forward to seeing our daughter and her date all decked out, to snapping her picture and adding a few more minutes to the video record of a childhood that seems to have passed in less time than it takes to view those tapes. As she steps into the limo, my wife and I will send her off not with nostalgic longing for the prom we never attended but for a childhood too quickly spent. How is it possible that not only our own school days are over but our daughter's as well? I'm not yet ready to give it all up.

Well, with any luck we'll get to enjoy the process one more time with grandchildren. In the meantime, I'm going to start saving for that future prom. If the past is any guide, a suburban unit won't even begin to cover it.

RARE SIGHTINGS

A year or two ago, or so I'm told, a neighbor spotted a white-tailed deer quietly grazing on the nearby elementary school playing field. It was one of those misty, early autumn mornings, a light ground fog drifting just above the grass, the corners of the field melting into white vapor. Apparently, the startled witness watched in wonder and disbelief for several minutes until convinced that the tawny deer was not some spectral visitation, then rushed home to summon a corroborating pair of eyes. By the time they returned, however, the rare visitor had fled, with no one to mark its flight.

I heard the story with some skepticism. I often encounter deer on my walks through up-county woodlands, but not once during my forty-three years in this village, not even in the seven-hundred-acre county park across town. And except for Red Maple Swamp, a two-acre tangle of honeysuckle and mulberry a block from the elementary school, there isn't anything remotely resembling wilderness in this neighborhood, not a golf course, not a nature preserve, not even a large private estate. And even the swamp is riven with wood-chip cushioned paths and bordered by backyards teeming with manicured lawns and barking dogs. In every direction the landscape only grows more congested with concrete, cars, and closely set homes, hardly the ideal environment for foraging deer.

Though rural neighborhoods to the north provide plenty of sanctuary and forage for deer, and residents regularly encounter them on back roads and in their gardens, this village offers little in the way of natural cover and virtually no access from up county, save a narrow bicycle corridor adjacent to the railroad and parkway. In places only a few yards wide and asphalt covered, it is anything but wild. Yet it does eventually lead to the protected watershed of the county reservoir. But why a deer would abandon the relative safety of those woods to wander six miles south, risking almost certain collision with trains and trucks, buses and cars, bicyclists, joggers, and walkers is anyone's guess? Out of curiosity? In search of adventure? Or thanks to a hopelessly tangled sense of direction? The more I thought about it, the more preposterous a deer just down the street began to seem.

Until yesterday, when, in an instant, my attitude about such sightings changed. I was sitting on the porch reading the Sunday paper when something larger than a squirrel, larger than a raccoon, larger even than the red-tailed hawks that occasionally perch in our white pines, wandered across the lawn. I watched in amazement as a wild turkey emerged from the shrubbery and paused a moment in the middle of the backyard. On my walks upstate I've often encountered them, usually in foraging flocks of four or five, their thick, ungainly bodies and red-tinged necks jerking forward and back as they probe the forest floor for acorns and beechnuts. At the first sight of hikers they bolt for cover, melting quickly into the brown underbrush. Like deer, they have the capacity to vanish into the wild almost instantly. So ubiquitous were they during colonial times that Benjamin Franklin facetiously proposed them as the national bird. But in time the wild turkey vanished from these precincts along with so many other species that had once populated the southern Hudson valley, migrating steadily northward ahead of suburban development.

Yet there, in seeming defiance of this two-hundred-year-old pattern of northward migration away from population centers, stood one bold or hopelessly disoriented turkey facing south. Spotting me standing open-mouthed at the edge of the porch, it seemed in no particular hurry to flee, remaining there even as I summoned my wife and children to join me, even as I retrieved my video camera and gingerly approached, eye glued to the viewfinder. It watched me near, then continued slowly toward the street, suffered a sudden change of heart at my neighbor's fence, turned back in the direction it had come, and began to pick up speed. Perhaps to intimidate me, or maybe just in readiness, it reared back a moment and spread its huge brown and white wings, flapping twice and growing momentarily light-footed before resuming its former graceless posture and scuttling off into the skunk cabbage and maple saplings of the nearby swamp.

Though capable of short bursts of flight, wild turkeys prefer to waddle to safety, and in all my northern encounters have done exactly that, sometimes with astonishing speed. Which is not to say that this turkey, like the ubiquitous geese that settle on every green sward in the village, couldn't have winged in from the north. But no matter how it arrived, the question remains: why did it bother? True, local property values have never been higher, the town's much-vaunted school system and its charges are thriving, all neighborhood dogs are confined behind steel or invisible electric fences, residents diligently recycle, beautify their lawns with flowering shrubs, and divide their vote almost equally between Republican and Democratic candidates. So why shouldn't any self-respecting turkey want to take up residence in this place we proudly call a village in a park?

Whatever the reason, I felt enormous joy at this brief sighting. It seemed to suggest that our local ecosystem is healthier than many believe, capable of sustaining not only ten-ton SUVs and their air-conditioned occupants, but unaccommodated wildlife as well. The neighborhood feels that much richer for the return of this former resident. We are custodians of so much more than simply our own comfort, entrusted with maintaining this extraordinary place we call home not just for ourselves but for all nature. The greatest testament to our successful discharge of that sacred trust is the return of those species that once populated this territory in abundance: turkey and pheasant; grouse and heron; eagle, hawk, and owl; beaver and porcupine; coyote and fox. To live alongside them would be to dwell not merely in a park, but in a garden—*the* garden. What greater legacy can we leave our children?

In the meantime, I'm keeping an eye out for that deer.

NEARLY NAKED POWER WALKING

From a block away it was apparent that something was different about this early morning walker. I'm accustomed to women power walking and jogging through the neighborhood in various states of undress; they do so every day, summer and winter, rain or shine. Some streak by in baggy T-shirts, some in sweats, some in glittery spandex. On the hottest days, with men running shirtless, high school girls occasionally strip down to sports bras and shorts, a pleasant reminder that Title IX has changed the landscape in more ways than one.

But last week I encountered something altogether new and wonderful. It was hot enough for a nearly naked encounter of the high school kind and for a moment, as I jogged toward the approaching silhouette, I assumed it was yet another teenage girl emulating World Cup soccer winner Brandi Chastain. But the black, calf-length tights were more in keeping with the attire of older joggers and something about them seemed slightly askew. The figure struck me as oddly hipless. Perhaps it was not a woman at all but a young man wearing a cut-off jersey and football pants, a trifle unconventional, to be sure, but not altogether beyond the pale. Indeed, that hipless midsection was beginning to look like a substantial beer belly, good reason for a nice long walk.

But no, the swinging, shoulder length hair coming into sharper focus suggested woman, and that bare mid-section was beginning to take on delightful new possibilities. Arms swinging with great deliberateness, she forged ahead on long, lean legs. This was no overweight football player. If anything her face looked a trifle gaunt, concave cheeks below prominent cheek bones. No, I realized as I jogged past, this early morning walker was pregnant, gloriously pregnant, one might almost say defiantly pregnant, easily in her seventh month, her naked belly as "out there" as Demi Moore on the cover of *Vanity Fair*. How times have changed.

It wasn't that long ago that women shrank from any public exposure of their expectancy, all but disappearing from view during their last trimester, and appearing, when they did, in clothes designed to conceal rather than celebrate their condition—maternity blouses and dresses ornamented with Peter Pan collars suggesting that the wearer was as androgynous as that fictional hero. For all the advances women were making in the workplace, they still accepted second-class status as bearers of children, removing themselves from the labor market early in pregnancy, from social events as their figures ballooned, even from everyday commerce, as though it were somehow unseemly for them to be seen in the supermarket or at the cleaners in their ninth month.

A generation ago single mothers were unheard of. We had instead "unwed mothers," unfortunate young women who had "gotten themselves pregnant," as though the condition were wholly self-inflicted, and who were gossiped about in whispered tones usually reserved for terminal illness. No right-thinking unmarried woman chose to have a child either naturally or artificially (not an option back then) and those compelled by fate to raise children alone were looked upon with compassion, dread, or derision. But certainly not envy. Pregnant high school girls were spirited away to distant relatives or special "homes" as soon as their "mistake" became obvious, and often returned to school months later as though nothing but an extended trip abroad had intervened. No one looked too closely into their eyes to discover the emotional consequences of adoption or abortion or miscarriage. Most simply preferred not to know.

And then it all began to change. Childbearing was suddenly cut lose from marriage. Men and women alike took to raising families singlehandedly. "Unwed mother" vanished from the lexicon, replaced by single mother, surrogate mother, midlife mother (and, less felicitously, teenage mother). Family underwent a stunning expansion, the term referring now to almost any combination of individuals of the same or opposite sex, the same or different generations, the same or different genes. Single mothers, infants strapped to their chests, began appearing in the workplace. So, too, single fathers. No shame was attached to these configurations, just expressions of amazement accompanied by a murmured, "It's a new world," along with sympathy for all the sleepless nights that lay ahead and the inevitable challenges posed by the effort to balance career and family responsibilities with no help from either partner or spouse.

And still, excepting Demi's famous pose and, more recently, a soaking wet Brooke Shields, images of highly pregnant women continue to be confined largely to the pages of *National Geographic*. Something about seeing a woman in her third trimester seems to unseat the unpregnant, arousing some primordial fear of suddenly finding ourselves drawn into the middle of an unscheduled birth experience. Summer spawns arresting states of undress among not just the super-trim but the heavily endowed, yet pregnant women still keep themselves largely under wraps and, when they do appear at the local pool, are often clad in flounced bathing costumes that bear a closer resemblance to Queen Victoria than Victoria's Secret.

When my wife was carrying our twins, she began to look deliverable in her fourth month. Every errand elicited expressions of amazement and apprehension, strangers offered their seats, questioned the wisdom of her being out and about in such a state, wondered how her Lamaze training was going, if her obstetrician was on call? Nervous taxi drivers assumed she was headed for the hospital. Growing weary of having to explain that her gestation was not as far along as it appeared, she took to wearing a small rhinestone pin that said, "Twins." For a time it allayed the worst fears, but there was no keeping pace with the astonishing growth of her babies. By the seventh month she was finding it difficult to slip in behind the steering wheel, by the eighth stairs became impossible without a helping hand pressed against her lower back. In her final month, even lying in bed was exhausting. But she was a glory, so exuberantly expectant that when she entered a room, the cantilevered twins proceeded her by several seconds and never failed to elicit exclamations of awe.

For pregnancy is nothing if not awe-inspiring, the central miracle of our existence. How much we lose in wonder and in simple gratitude by concealing it from view. So the other day I considered turning back to tell that pregnant, nearly naked power walker how beautiful she looked and how much I admired her for being so comfortable in her own pregnant skin; but she didn't need my approbation or support, I realized, she just needed fresh air and movement and the company of her own thoughts. She already seemed to know what a blessing it was to be carrying a child and to be in good health and capable of race-walking the neighborhood on a hot day wearing almost nothing and loving it.

COLLEGE BOUND

There would be no tears, I told myself. After all, she'd spent last summer traveling through Europe, the summer before touring Israel, and for four years had attended sleep-away camp. We were used to her long absences, had even come to enjoy the idea of being on our own after so many years of child confinement—no needy kids to rush home to, no expensive babysitters, just two places set for dinner and our own wishes to fulfill.

So as we packed the rental van with our daughter's most prized possessions and prepared to drive her to college I thought, this won't be so tough; she's eager to begin the next phase of her life and we're delighted she has reached this milestone. Then too, our nest was not yet empty; her younger brother and sister were home for another two years. And it wasn't as though she were flying off to Chicago or LA. She'd be near enough to return for the weekend, if she cared to, and there was always the telephone. No, this wouldn't be difficult at all, I reasoned. What I hadn't counted on was my heart.

Did I mention she's my firstborn, that for the first six months of her life she was out of my arms only long enough to nurse, and even then I hovered nearby, utterly in thrall to the miracle of her existence, that the only way she seemed able to fall asleep was clutched to my chest on long walks around the neighborhood, that the moment she entered our lives everything paled to insignificance beside her infant accomplishments and well-being. For the next eighteen years one could take my temperature by her moods: when she was cheerful I felt light-hearted, when depressed or angry, my outlook turned cloudy. This was the child I was going to send from home for the next four years—if not for

a lifetime—without a pang, without a tear, without a terrible wrenching of my heart? Oh, silly man!

Still, I got almost as far as goodbye that afternoon before I realized
my mistake. We made the drive in high spirits, unloaded the van with
the help of a small army of exuberant upperclassmen, picnicked with
several hundred parents and their nervous-eyed freshmen, hung pic-
tures and posters, unpacked suitcases, made the bed, installed the computer, and through it all kept up our cheerful banter, delighting in the
newness of her environment and the echoes it evoked of our own college experience thirty years ago. Who had time to be broken-hearted
when there were so many new people to meet, schedules and routines
to learn, campus buildings to find, books to buy, social plans to make?
The day hurried by, taken up with a welter of activities that ended with
an address by the college president in the university chapel. We listened as he recounted separation tales of his own, smiling at the univer-
sality of our experience. But when he said, "Soon you'll be saying
goodbye to your son or daughter," it finally hit me: This wasn't just
another exploratory campus visit; this time she wasn't coming home.

A handful of small tasks remained and then, finally, it was time to
load the empty suitcases back into the van and say our goodbyes. I suc-
ceeded in maintaining my composure until my daughter clung to me
as she hadn't clung since childhood, with a palpable longing for the
protective embrace of her father and for a past that was ending at that
very moment for us all. "I love you, Dad," she murmured into my
chest. The hand that stroked her hair was the same palm that had cradled her infant head just moments ago. I blinked away tears and managed a crooked smile, uttering cheerful words of reassurance meant as
much for me as for her: "You're going to love it here: so many new
people to meet, ideas to explore. And we're just a phone call away."
Then she embraced her mother and the two of them dissolved in tears.

All around us young men and women were saying goodbye to their
parents, looking less like confident college students than bewildered
children. Finally, in a moment of bravery, our daughter released her

mother and stepped to the curb. "I love you guys," she called as the car backed away, then waved until we were out of sight, the amber light glistening in her wet eyes.

"She'll be fine," I insisted, trying to ease my own ache as well as my wife's. "She'll be just fine."

But how would I be? For the first several days I kept finding myself in her room, wandering from dresser to desk to closet, taking note of all that was gone, surveying all that she had left behind. There, in the center of her bookcase, stood the high school diploma she had proudly received just two months before, beside it four thick high school yearbooks, the three thinner ones from middle school, her elementary school folders, and stacks of spiral notebooks and loose-leaf binders. How was it possible that those twelve intense, miraculous years of schooling had come to a close, that she would no longer call home at 3:00 asking to be picked up, no longer keep the phone line tied up half the night, no longer set the wall between her room and ours vibrating with her music? Her bedroom, far too tidy now, had become the vague cipher of a former life, lacking the energetic disarray of her exuberant personality. And every time the young father down the street passed with his infant daughter in his arms, I longed for the past.

Instead of lessening with time, the pain of separation seemed to intensify, as though my heart were only just beginning to comprehend what reason had long since understood—she wasn't coming home. Late one night, feeling particularly bereft, I began searching the Internet for an old song I thought would lift my spirits. I had heard it only once, but remembered the occasion with particular vividness. I was driving my daughter to school, listening to her complaints about excessive homework and burdensome tests when a new version of the old Sam Cooke song, "What a Wonderful World," came on the radio. In an effort to brighten her mood I began to sing along. At first she turned away, annoyed by my antics, but then she began to take note of the lyrics—"Don't know much about history, don't know much biology"—turned back and smiled.

Why it came to me this night so many years later I don't know, but I needed to hear it and with the help of the internet was able to download and play it. Delighted by my discovery, I ran upstairs to share it with my daughter, realizing halfway there that I couldn't. Was this how it would be from now on, communion forever denied, the present moment always unfulfilled? Wistfully, I emailed her, telling her how much I missed her and reminding her of the time we had heard the song together. I attached the music file to my electronic note and sent it on its way. Several minutes later my computer rang with notice of incoming mail. My daughter wrote:

> Dear Dad,
>
> That song you sent me was so nice! I've been thinking a lot about how weird it is that I don't live at home anymore. I'm actually on my own, but not really, because I know I can always call you or go home whenever I need to.
>
> School is getting better all the time but I can't wait to see you next weekend. Tell everyone I say hello. I love you!!!
>
> Your first born

She seemed, if not quite back in my arms, very close to my heart, sharing not only my wistfulness, but the comfort I took from an old song and from a memory of our shared past. I realized in that moment how close we remained, how deeply connected despite the miles. What had seemed an unbridgeable chasm was nothing more than air. Our separation was one of distance, not of spirit. And for the moment that was solace enough.

LAST LEAF

From my window I look across frozen lawns to the woods beyond, searching for color, for brilliant hues up in the highest reaches, for the red and gold glory of autumn. But the maples and oaks are bare now, stripped clean during the night by a high wind that put an end to the celebration, ushering in this somber, gray prelude to winter. Gone is the blaze and snap of October when each tree emerged briefly from the ubiquitous green backdrop of summer for an incandescent interval of gaudy pageantry, like old men suddenly taken to wearing plaid trousers, old women arrayed in lavender and ribbons, making one last heartrending bid for recognition before succumbing to the dull sameness of death. During the night the carnival of color folded its tents and fled south, leaving behind the muddy midway and the colorless debris of spent festivity. And now what?

Where is the joy that accompanied every sweep of the eye, that animated every tree and shrub at street corner, park, and school yard, turning the warm green light of summer into the arresting red dazzle of fall—our sole consolation for the loss of languid August days and cricket-filled nights? The woods are silent now, gray branches against a gray sky, the forest floor slowly decomposing, absorbing all that fallen color into a rich brown humus that blankets rocks and roots and floats for a time upon the black waters of woodland streams. Nothing stirs but foraging squirrels and chipmunks. All the birds seem to have flown before the cold gusts that continue to rattle the tree trunks, wrenching free the few remaining yellow leaves to spin and twirl their way to oblivion.

There's haunting drama in all this, the drama of transition, of the sudden clarity that comes from loss and newfound simplicity. Every day the palette changes, the landscape reinvents itself. But soon the drama ends. The kinetic energy stored in every suspended leaf is consumed in its final whirling dance, the bright hues leach back into the soil, even the fresh brown carpet turns to dust, leaving only longing. In the great crucible of autumn are ground all the ingredients of eternity—the fall from glory, the memory of greatness, the promise of rebirth—awaiting that moment in late March when the earth shakes off repose and regenerates itself.

Yet look hard enough, piercing the forward picket of dormant tree trunks, and you may light upon a single reluctant sapling, a misplaced beech among the maples, oaks, and pines, standing no taller than a boy of fourteen, and like that boy, reluctant to kneel before the stern dictates of late autumn's authority. Its tan leaves still cling to spindly branches and, if the past is any guide, will continue to do so even through the harshest winter storms, bleached white by wind and an unnatural endurance, growing gradually translucent, adding an unfamiliar clicking to the winter wind, like the chatter of frozen teeth. Occasionally the rebel is an oak, soaring sixty or eighty feet into the air, its broad canopy of leaves a gnarled and wrinkled brown that refuses to succumb to the inevitable fall until assured by spring that new growth is imminent. This is not the intentional goading and posturing of youth, but the mute stubbornness of a tannin-saturated old age.

I love those trees, both the young and the old, for their parchment defiance, their resistance to uniformity, proof not only that nature cultivates and admits exception, but that there is great beauty in decay. Nothing about the retention of desiccated leaves makes biological sense—dormant trees need to conserve their resources when the sun is too low and the days too short for effective photosynthesis, and do so by shedding their foliage. Yet still these renegades endure, scattered throughout the woods, biological scapegraces brandishing the flag of a fallen empire, out of time, out of step, refusing to accept the inevitable end that the waning light and rising cold have dictated. Let death come, if it must, they seem to declare, we will not release our hold on all that we cherish. Rather than put away their dead and dying, they hold fast. And in the harsh winter wind they promenade, albeit stiffly, with the somber elegance of eternity.

At twilight I leave my desk and walk through the woods. The bitter winds have ebbed; a purple light domes the trees; frost is gathering in the hollows. Underfoot the carpet of moldering leaves crackles. Before me a single beech sapling stands wrapped in a copper haze, pale leaves hanging in fluttering clusters, catching even the faintest breath of wind. They are never still, even in death. The gray-black bark of the young tree is smooth and elastic, unmarred by age; the leaves are ribbed and wrinkled, the edges curled by drought. A cold gust cuts through the woods. The naked maples barely register the wind, but the beech bursts into a russet flurry, each leaf quivering and chattering. Here youth clings to old age, old age holds fast to youth. Together they will dance through this cold season, animating the lifeless woods, punctuating the austere beauty of dormancy with their defiant waltz.

Quietly the dark descends, the cold deepens. The long, lovely night of winter is just beginning.

DRIVING WITH DAVID

I'm rediscovering village streets I'd forgotten existed, narrow private drives and cul-de-sacs one would normally have no occasion to visit if not calling upon someone in the immediate neighborhood—unless, of course, you are seated beside your sixteen-year-old son, the ink still wet on his learner's permit as he explores every nook and cranny in a manic effort to scent-mark all the known world with his tires and declare it his own. Born in December, he has watched all his friends and class-mates earn not only junior but, in some cases, senior licenses while he has waited none-too-patiently on the sidelines, ruing the month of his birth. But now, finally, it's his turn and he is determined to log as many miles in the next few weeks as his friends accumulated during the past year. Every time the phone rings I expect his sugared voice on the other end asking, "Feel like taking a spin after school with your boy?" How can I say no? In all likelihood this is the last time he's going to need me in this way, the last time he's going to rely on my expertise, the last time he's going to truly crave my company—well, mine and my car.

Three years ago his older sister was just as eager to drive, so eager in fact, that against my better judgment she took and passed her road test three weeks after receiving her permit. His twin sister, however, is quite another species. She's still prone to ask, after a year of occasional prac-tice in the driveway, "Remind me again: which is the gas and which is the brake?" You'll understand, therefore, why I feel somewhat less secure in the passenger seat with her at the wheel, and why I've encour-aged her, no matter what the cost, to seek professional instruction in a car with an auxiliary brake. The first time she drove me around the block, she made a left turn and asked, "Which side of the street am I supposed to be on now?" A huge UPS truck was bearing down upon us at the time. Blessedly, it stopped; we stopped. I drove the rest of the way home.

Her brother, on the other hand, seems born to drive. For a year he practiced in his grandmother's driveway, accelerating down the straightaway, whipping around the tight circle by the front door, then racing back toward the street, stopping within inches of the pavement, heart pounding, eyes and heart fixed on the great asphalt beyond. The temptation to pierce the invisible barrier imposed by law must have been formidable, but he never let it overwhelm his judgment, chastened by stories of his uncle who careened around that same circle almost forty years before and one day decided to see what lay beyond self-restraint. He returned home between two police officers and didn't see the inside of a car for months.

So as we left the Department of Motor Vehicles with learner's permit in hand, David asked for the keys and drove the ten miles home, negotiating the congestion of downtown Yonkers and the mayhem of Central Avenue as though he'd been doing so for months. Only once did I find myself inching over toward the center console as a passing truck forced him almost against the curb, but the rest of the trip proved blessedly uneventful. Since then we've spent hours side by side, running errands, driving to school, parallel parking on local streets. Do I enjoy endlessly circling the neighborhood, checking side-view mirrors, constantly glancing over my shoulder, worrying about every other car on the road in addition to ours? Not really. But I know this is it, that in a matter of weeks he will achieve the independence that only a driver's license can bestow. Never mind Bar Mitzvah or Confirmation. Driving is the true beginning of adulthood.

Less than a week into this new routine David asks if we can drive on the parkway. I hesitate. The faster we go the less time there is to correct a potentially fatal mistake. "I've got to learn sometime," he insists. I try to divert him with a little more parallel parking, but he slips in and out of spaces effortlessly and soon grows bored. "Come on, Dad, the parkway," he urges. Fortunately, most of the fastest and most dangerous highways are off-limits to permit holders, but the one closest to home is not.

"You haven't even been driving a week," I remind him.

"But I've got good instincts," he insists.

"There is no such thing as an instinct for driving," I tell him. If there were, none of us would ever get behind the wheel. Peer over the edge of a ten-story building or a hundred foot cliff and we instinctively back away, sensing danger. Height we have an instinct for, not speed. We feel nothing at sixty miles per hour, nothing even at 600. We sense only acceleration and, unfortunately, it exhilarates rather than frightens us. How can I get this teenage boy to appreciate the danger inherent in that thrilling press of the accelerator, the roar of the engine, the sudden lurch backward in the seat? What keeps us alive out there on the road is not instinct, I tell him, but experience, judgment, and reflexes—none of which is innate. If they were, car rentals would not categorically reject all drivers under twenty-five and insurance companies would not double and triple premiums for adolescent drivers. Their claim records tell a simple tale: it takes roughly nine years for drivers to acquire the necessary skills to keep out of trouble. Almost half of all sixteen year olds will be involved in an accident during their first year behind the wheel. It's a chilling statistic. And if that is true after six or ten months of driving, how much more so just six days out.

But cowardice in a teacher is inexcusable. I taught him to cross the street safely, to swim, to ride a bike. It behooves me to usher him into this new arena as well. So I remind him again of the first thing I said when I handed him the keys outside the Department of Motor Vehicles: "You now have the power to do serious damage. One small error of judgment, one moment of inattention, one ill-advised race down a local street could end in tragedy."

"I understand," he says with adult forbearance, resisting the impulse to remind me how often I've told him the same thing. So I don't repeat the stories from my own childhood of the drag race across Olmsted

Road that landed two kids in the hospital with severe internal injuries and multiple broken bones, the fatal crash at Brewster and Harcourt, the pedestrian fatality at Post and Huntington. There but for the grace of God go all of us, it seems. We are never so vulnerable as when we are behind the wheel. It chills me to think of the risks that await my children.

"All right, to the parkway," I finally reply. Better to experience it with me beside him now than on his own later, I reason. Cautiously, but confidently, he merges with traffic and gets us up to speed. My feet press a little more firmly against the floor mat, my hands clasp my knees. The guard rail seems dangerously close. I suppress the impulse to flinch, to cry out. My eyes dart to the mirrors, to the road ahead. Surely he is going too fast. But he's not and gradually I relax, reassured by his confident control as he settles back into the seat, checks mirrors and speedometer, signals to change lanes, looks over his shoulder, and smiles at the thought that he's driving on the highway. "Doesn't really feel any different than thirty," he remarks. "But it's a rush getting up to speed."

Yes it is, I have to admit. And that's what worries me. Testosterone and gasoline are a potentially fatal mix. But just as I'm about to make the point, a silver Porsche streaks by at half the speed of light, piloted by a balding man in bifocals who should know better. David's eyes follow longingly. It's not just testosterone, it's the culture.

Half an hour later we pull into the driveway. "Well done," I tell him as he maneuvers into the garage.

"Same time tomorrow?" he asks, already aching to be back behind the wheel.

"We'll see," I hedge.

He takes one last adoring look at the dashboard, pats the steering wheel, and declares, "Nice ride!" then reluctantly opens the door and stands a moment beside the car, not quite believing that this is his life, that all the years of waiting are finally behind him, that he's only a few short weeks away from complete independence. And then, as though ambivalent about that very freedom, he throws his arms around me and lays his head on my shoulder. "Thank you, Daddy," he murmurs.

"You done good, kiddo," I tell him. And then I take him by the shoulders and make one final plea for caution. "Just remember, you're the guardian of my grandchildren. Be safe."

"I promise," he replies, then bounds up the steps to the house shouting, "I love driving!" May God protect him.

LOVE AT FIRST SIGHT

It wasn't just the freshly scrubbed faces of all those high school aspirants and the equally youthful undergraduate tour guides that conspired to make me feel so old and out of place as we toured a dozen college campuses recently, the dormant landscape itself seemed to reverberate with the same plangent observation—you're not a kid anymore. Upstate, the glistening brown pate of each barren hillock and ridge gleamed through the bare trees like the receding hairline of middle age, reminding me that, jeans, sweatshirt, and sneakers notwithstanding, I was not likely to be mistaken for a prospective student, and neither would the other tired-eyed, footsore parents schlepping their eager, anxious high school juniors across quads and through dorms in search of the perfect fit, their next home, the beginning of the rest of their lives. And perhaps it was just as well: three decades after my own college experience, I still didn't know how best to set about finding the right school for myself or my children.

Though we came well prepared, arriving at each destination armed with sheaves of Internet notes, campus maps, and probing questions, I soon realized that this process was as alchemical, as mysterious as love itself. Somehow, on the basis of a course catalogue, a pile of professionally produced propaganda, and a few hours spent roaming through cafeterias, classrooms, and libraries, sixteen and seventeen year olds are expected to make an informed choice about their future, a choice that will effect not only what they do with the rest of their lives but, very possibly, who they spend their lives with. A wisteria arbor, a glistening cupola, a basketball court, or a tone of voice can tip the balance. So too a high wind, deep snow, a drenching downpour. Our older daughter insists she knew the moment she stepped from the car that she had found her future school. What had made her so certain? She simply felt at home, she said. To assure herself it wasn't just some trick of the light or an odd moment of vulnerability, she returned three times, staying overnight, attending classes, talking with undergraduates. Whatever it was continued to call out to her, she applied early, and fortunately had her affections returned by the admissions office. A year later she remains convinced of the rightness of her first impression. Would our twins be as lucky?

During the course of a week we walked through vest-pocket colleges and colossal university campuses, drove from remote villages surrounded by acres of wilted corn to soot-begrimed cityscapes merging dormitory and downtown in a seamless continuum of concrete, brick, and glass. We joined small tours of perspective students and jostling herds of the hopeful, spoke to undergraduates and professors, admissions officers and alumni, local residents and shopkeepers, waiters and waitresses hoping to gain insight and confirm or refute our first impressions. We rarely came away indifferent, usually provoked by setting, spiel, and students to a powerful and sometimes quantifiable verdict.

But were those reactions built upon anything more substantial than sand? What did we really know beyond what we gleaned from professional salespeople and observations colored by personal bias? Show me Gothic stone and colonial brick and my response is likely to be favorable. Walk me through unvarnished concrete and glass and I'm inclined to look elsewhere. And yet, what do these architectural details tell us about the quality of teaching that takes place within their walls? What do they say about faculty commitment to students, administrative commitment to faculty, student commitment to studies, about binge drinking, drug abuse, sexual harassment? Can one assess the general health of a community or the rightness of such an environment for one's child based on a quick walk-through and the purchase of a T-shirt at the campus bookstore? I doubt it. But that doesn't prevent us from trying.

Hurtling across the brown landscape of upstate New York and New England, we gave physical form to names we knew solely by reputation: the huge university consisting of a dozen separate colleges, the small liberal arts institution know for its pedagogic radicalism, the renowned research facility, the party school, the sports magnet. Gratifying as it was to put a face to a name, we wondered what truly lurked behind those beguiling eyes. In the car, afterwards, we pooled our observations, attempting to broaden the twins' perspective and enlarge their field of view. They had left home with definite notions of what they sought in a four-year college: for one, mid-size to large, possibly urban, definitely not rural; for the other mid-size to small, possibly rural or suburban, definitely not urban. But by the end of the first day they had both fallen in love with the same small, remote college and the same sprawling city university, realizing how incomplete their notions of each had been.

Two days later they came away disappointed by a school they had been predisposed by hearsay and guidance counselors to love. What was the source of their disenchantment, I asked. They struggled to give it a name: something in the air, an aloofness, an apparent indifference communicated by the tone of the tour guide, by the receptionist in the admissions office, by chance conversations, by the very landscape. In this instance, I shared their feeling. But was it justified?

I knew something of the place, having spent three semesters there over thirty years ago, and wondered if this return visit would corroborate or contradict my earlier impressions. I kept my feelings to myself, expecting to see it with different eyes, to appreciate qualities that had eluded me as an undergraduate. And given enough time I might have, but in the two hours we spent touring my old haunts, talking to undergraduates, listening to an admissions officer, I was left with a melancholy feeling of déjà vu: this was simply not a nurturing environment. If only I had listened to my own heart thirty years ago instead of following the dictates of my dean and of fashion. Perhaps our first impressions aren't so wrong-headed after all, less the product of wishful thinking and misconception than of second sight, sensitivity, and judicious caution.

Five days and twelve hundred miles later we returned home struggling to remember the names of all the schools we'd visited and one or two salient characteristics of each. The twins had embarked on the tour knowing nothing of college life beyond what their older sister had told them. They now possessed a sizeable portfolio of personal encounters to help them select the school that might be home to them for four years. It seems a daunting prospect at any age; so much hangs in the balance. A part of me would have welcomed the chance to relive that transformative experience with an adult appreciation of its manifold opportunities, but the staid fifty year old lurking behind sneakers and jeans whispered, "It's their turn now, thank goodness." In the end I was content to let them haul the two tons of course catalogues and come-ons up to their rooms to begin the process of deciding what they wanted to do with the rest of their lives, knowing full well that their love might prove unrequited, that the days ahead were fraught with uncertainty.

HOW LITTLE WE KNOW

For years I knew her and her husband only as fellow singers in our community chorus, distant neighbors with whom I shared an interest in music and the collegiality of performance. We exchanged smiles and choral news whenever our paths crossed at the supermarket or bank, and occasionally discussed getting together for dinner, but nearly ten years passed before we set a date. And when that night finally arrived I wondered if we had enough in common to sustain an entire evening of conversation.

I needn't have worried. After the usual pleasantries, we launched into our life stories, each describing in turn how we'd come to live in the village. And while this was engaging in the way of all first encounters—the unanticipated forces that place people of disparate backgrounds side by side in towns far from birthplace or ancestry—it grew astonishing as our neighbor revealed just how far she had traveled to reach this table. I came away stunned by her story and the quiet revelation that this unassuming, soft-spoken woman was obliquely related to one of the most famous writers of the 20th century.

From my first encounter I had noticed something faintly exotic about her face that belied her unaccented English, blond hair, and suburban dress. In fact, she had not been born in the upstate New York of her childhood but in Asia, arriving in America as an infant, a refugee of war. Her mother, still living, was Chinese. Her father, of German and Dutch descent, had died almost thirty years ago in his mid-eighties. A rough calculation suggested he was well into middle age by the time she was born.

Had we been better acquainted, I might have overwhelmed her with questions about her past: what had she learned of her mother's culture,

language, and arts; what had brought her father to China almost a century ago; what commonalities of temperament and thought had united
two people of such divergent cultures? Had she ever considered how
different her life might have been had war not forced them to leave her
homeland, ever returned to the place of her birth, ever met her Asian
relatives, ever thought of moving back?

Sensing my interest, she revealed that her mother had not been her
father's first wife. He had been married for almost twenty years to an
American woman. "You might find this interesting," she said without
pretense, "though an awful lot of people today don't know who I'm
talking about." And then she revealed who that first wife had been,
once the most famous woman writer in the world, credited with singlehandedly awakening broad western interest in Asian culture, a mission-
ary's daughter who had dined with kings and presidents, received the
Nobel Prize, been translated into scores of languages and celebrated
not only for her writing but her humanitarian efforts around the globe.
Seventy years ago she had been known to virtually every reader and
school child, but today few recognized her name and fewer still read
her books. The woman was Pearl Buck.

We didn't talk about literature that night, for our neighbor admitted that she had never been able to separate the writer from the wife
who had played such a large and ultimately unhappy role in her
father's early life. Though she had never met her, she had heard many
unflattering tales over the years, angry anecdotes born of the residue of
hard feelings that any separation and divorce engender. So she spoke
instead of those feelings, still so vivid, of her mother's durable antago-
nism, of the child born to that first union and the many children
adopted by the author after she remarried, children our neighbor had
never met, yet who shared an odd and ill-defined connection to her.
What does one call a parent's first spouse, or the children of that
spouse and a subsequent partner, I wondered. To our neighbor they
were all part of another time and place, that vanished world between

the wars that had spawned so many astonishing artists and so many unhappy marriages, her father's among them.

Did she regret never meeting the famous author, I asked. Not really, she replied. But once in childhood her father had taken her to visit the only child of that first union, now grey-haired and living under the care of nurses. So many years separated them that it was hard for the little girl to look upon this adult as her half-sister. She seemed rather some distant, maiden aunt. Years later she learned the woman had died but admitted to feeling little sense of personal loss. By then her father was long dead and so too the author. Gradually the celebrated name faded from view, the only residue being one well-remembered if now unread book, *The Good Earth*, and the classic movie it spawned. Yet that night she seemed to live anew through our neighbor, a woman she had never met but whom fate had cast as half-sister to her only child.

When we returned home I pulled the Pulitzer Prize-winning novel from the shelf and began to reread it, realizing how deserving it was of the praise once received. How much more vital it seemed in the afterglow of the discovery that my quiet musical colleague was so deeply and unexpectedly connected to a story set in a world long gone by a woman who was once a household name. How little we know of the astounding tales our very neighbors embody.

THE DOCTOR IS IN

Now that doctors no longer make house calls, my neighbor said, she was glad to be beyond child rearing. What would she have done without the reassuring visits of the family pediatrician during all those childhood illness, the endless round of measles, mumps, and chicken pox, the viruses, flu, and strep that routinely swept through the house? She still remembered the time her youngest son's fever climbed dangerously above 106 degrees, the doctor arriving at 1:00 a.m. to administer penicillin and help sponge the boy's beet-red body through that interminable night. She marveled at the young mothers who routinely bundled their feverish children into cars and drove long distances through all weather to wait in crowded, over-heated doctor's offices full of other sick children. An ailing child belonged in bed, she insisted, and who should better understand that than a pediatrician?

I smiled at the notion. Even before the days of managed care, the idea of a busy physician wasting precious time traveling from patient to patient rather than treating them rapidly and efficiently in a well-appointed office, seemed not only obsolete but unwise. Now with HMOs, EPOs, and PPOs all but driving a stake through the heart of the once sacred doctor-patient relationship, transforming patients into "clients" and visits into "encounters," who expects anything remotely resembling personal care? And yet, one vestige of that kinder, gentler era still survives and a fortunate few are its beneficiaries.

Twenty years ago, expecting our first child, my wife and I discovered a local pediatric practice whose four physicians, while not accustomed to making house calls, nevertheless sat by the phone most mornings from 7:45 to 8:30 answering parents' anxious questions, evaluating symptoms, and scheduling emergency office visits when necessary. Any child who developed a fever during the night or awoke in pain could be tended to quickly and a parent's worst fears allayed. For two decades, the promise and practice of that access has saved our children from needless suffering and repeatedly eased our minds.

So it was with my neighbor's sense of dismay that I listened to friends recently tell of pediatricians who could only be reached through answering services, and often took hours to respond to fretful calls. Was it possible that the access we depended on—the early morning consultations that evaluated the sore throat for strep, the sprain for a break, the irritated eye for conjunctivitis, the cough for pneumonia—was going the way of house calls? Fewer doctors, it seemed, were willing to provide that critical access and fewer parents expected it, resolved to live with the anxieties built into modern medicine. With patient rosters numbering in the thousands, what physician had the time or energy to respond to every spontaneous appeal?

Our oldest is now nineteen and talks occasionally of finding her own internist, but whenever she's home and awakens with a bad cough or an infected ear, her first thought and ours is of the pediatrician who knows her so well and who we know will answer his phone at 7:45 and set about immediately to remedy her condition. Who would willingly relinquish such precious care, especially when the attachment goes so much deeper than mere convenience or gratitude.

Elizabeth was born without complication in a small labor room attended by her parents, a nurse, and an obstetrician. Our twins arrived under a wholly different constellation. Instead of one obstetrician there were two, instead of one nurse, three, and instead of a labor room, we all crowded into surgery, joined there by an anesthesiologist and our pediatrician. I wondered at the need for so many hands, but as the delivery progressed they all became crucial. While one obstetrician prepared to receive the first twin, the other was readying the second, rapidly maneuvering her out of a transverse position as soon as our son was born. After nine interminable months of gestation, every second now seemed critical. Second twins, we knew, run the risk of oxygen deprivation. So while nurses and doctors were ministering to my wife, and the anesthesiologist was monitoring her vital signs and those of our unborn twin, our pediatrician was quietly evaluating David, clearing his infant lungs, placing drops in his astonished eyes, checking his reflexes, listening to his heart. With my attention darting from newborn son to wife to the child still in utero, I heard him pronounce David in perfect health. I wanted to hug him.

Instead I hugged my freshly swaddled baby boy and awaited his twin. It was then that I began to understand why so many forces had been summoned. My wife, exhausted by David's birth, suddenly needed oxygen to carry on, as well as the practiced hands of two obstetricians working in tandem to position and engage her second baby. When our daughter finally slipped into the light, she did so with terrifying stillness, her skin pale blue. David had declared his birth with an instantaneous cry, but Juliana lay limp in the obstetrician's hands. She passed rapidly to the pediatrician in whose adroit care she blossomed pink and boisterous. My momentary panic subsided, relieved by an onrush of joy. But later that night I remembered my fleeting terror at the prospect of losing her, and recalled the wave of gratitude that washed over me as our pediatrician's deft hands coaxed her back into life.

For this and for the two decades of devoted care that have seen our children through illness and emergency to young adulthood, we owe him a debt beyond reckoning. For years I have meant to express that gratitude formally. How easy it would have been to write a note after yet another early morning call lay our most recent fears to rest. But I have been remiss. After the anxiety passes and the child recovers, I quickly forget how apprehensive and inept I feel when my children stumble into our bedroom, feverish or nauseated, head throbbing or muscles aching, asking what they should do, what I can do to relieve their symptoms.

So much superstition clings to issues of health. We knock wood and thank God when discussing the well-being of loved ones, feeling especially vulnerable to the malign forces that rain down illness, believing, there but for the grace of God.... Healthy, we pass doctors' offices with bated breath, like children skirting cemeteries. Perhaps that accounts for my negligence, the almost universal reluctance to think of doctors and illness except when compelled to do so. But my gratitude is no less for this lapse. I sleep more soundly knowing, come what may, that my children will be well cared for.

I only hope they are as fortunate in their physicians when their own children come along. Nothing has so eased our passage through parenthood as the knowledge that this ministering angel lies within easy reach whenever the need arises. We have been blessed. Thank you, Herb.

SILENT BEAUTY

When the power failed we were walking the beach at the eastern tip of Long Island, watching waves crash and slide across the sand, blessedly disconnected from the usual routines and preoccupations of life. Our days there had been bracingly elemental, reduced to little more than sun, sand, water, and wind; our sun-bleached eyes grown accustomed to a simple spectrum of white, blue, and green. So we didn't realize that anything was amiss until we returned to our beachside rooms and noticed a small crowd of hotel guests surrounding a portable radio perched on a picnic table. Most of the northeast was without electricity, we quickly learned, eight states and two Canadian provinces, from New Jersey to Ottawa and as far west as Michigan. And no one knew the cause.

The deeply tanned faces of our neighbors expressed both bemusement and worry. A few looked vaguely shell-shocked, unprepared for this sudden jolt of reality after so many carefree days at the beach. Someone mentioned terrorism, another nuclear meltdown. I simply thought: of all the places to find oneself in the midst of a power failure, surely an airy room at the beach in the middle of August ranked as extraordinarily fortunate. While city residents coped with stalled elevators and subways, inoperative stop lights, gridlocked intersections, and swarms of bewildered pedestrians wondering how best to get home, we had only to consider our dinner plans.

A few quick-thinking guests jumped into their cars in search of flashlights, batteries, and food while others, realizing that hot water would soon be scarce, hurried to the shower. But most simply returned to the beach with a renewed sense of their good fortune. There, beyond the dunes, it began to feel like a time out of time, uncorseted by the usual restraints of energy-dependent routines. The clocks had stopped, the lights were out, even the ubiquitous drone of air conditioners had ceased. Lacking refrigeration, most restaurants would have to close. The movie houses would be shuttered along with other beachside entertainments. We were released from even the petty tyranny of self-imposed amusements. Nature alone remained undisturbed by this sudden change and we were perfectly positioned to enjoy it.

But my wife was finding it hard to do so, concerned about patients on life-support, people trapped in high rises, all that spoiled food. She feared for national security, for planes in flight, and for our own home, suddenly vulnerable without electricity's vigilant eye. And the kids announced that they would feel less unsettled this lightless night in their own beds, no matter how hot it got. I tried to convince them that a three-hour drive along unlit highways through towns without functioning stop lights or gas stations, across bridges without operational tolls, simply to return to a dark house, certain to be less comfortable than our oceanside rooms, made little sense. I left unspoken the hope that, lacking electricity, our family vacation might finally become the one I had envisioned, stripped bare of the usual distractions, no televisions or VCRs, cell phones or CD players, just the beach and the sea and each other.

And then the neighbors on either side returned with pizzas, hot dogs, and charcoal, and invited us to join them in an impromptu barbeque. All doors were thrown wide, introductions were made, a warm collegiality developed. Families gathered around candle-lit picnic tables beside the dunes, adding their perishables to the mix, feeling like Swiss Families Robinson, gamely confronting a primal world of unrelieved darkness with ingenuity and good humor.

As the light began to fade we shared tales of previous blackouts: the stifling July night my wife and I spent spritzing each other with a plant mister in an airless apartment twenty-six years ago, and the more ominous outage in the mid-sixties, when, fearing Russian attack, we tuned in Walter Conkrite on a battery-powered TV, my father chuckling over this corroboration of one of his favorite quips, "If it weren't for Edison, we'd all be watching TV by candlelight."

Though we had been at the beach almost a week, the kids had not ventured out beyond the dunes after dark, unwilling to leave the cool, incandescent comfort of our rooms for the sultry, unlit shore. But now the transition was effortless, our eyes already adjusted to the dark, the narrow dune path easy to negotiate by starlight. We were greeted by a beach bristling with sparks. Small bonfires burned up and down the coast, surrounded by families roasting hot dogs and marshmallows in the yellow, wind-tossed flames.

Overhead the constellations sparkled with rare clarity amid a backwash of stars normally invisible in the ambient light of the suburbs. A single comet streaked through space, Scorpius curled against the usually indistinct contours of the Milky Way, Mars glowed a warm orange, and then the rust-red moon rose out of the ocean, casting pale silver shadows across the sand.

I felt renewed astonishment at the mysterious depths of the night sky. When one can command light at the flip of a switch, what difference does a sunrise make? But when the only light comes from the heavens, the advent of an evening moon or the sun at dawn is cause for celebration, anticipated almost as eagerly as childbirth, its effect immediate and profound.

I watched this celestial show with my back to the dunes until a sudden flicker of light caused me to turn. A faint white aura hung above the black silhouette of the heaped-up sand. The lights had returned. As I crossed the dunes the roar of the waves was replaced by the cicadalike drone of air conditioners. I felt faintly mournful at the loss of the boundless dark fraternity of the heavens. Already the twinkling canopy and moon-cast shadows had dimmed, obscured by the high-intensity glare of security lights.

The kids headed straight for the television, tuning in startling images of darkened skyscrapers silhouetted by canyoned streams of headlights. Within minutes they were back on their cell phones, talking to friends at home still without power.

"Good thing we didn't try to make the drive," they conceded, lounging in the frigid wash of the air conditioner. I was beginning to feel just the opposite: At home we would have been gifted with a few more lightless hours in the silent company of the stars.

IF WE ONLY KNEW THEN

During those first frenzied weeks after the twins were born, with three children under the age of three making certain that no one slept for longer than fifteen minutes and every waking moment was spent with at least one hungry, howling child in arms, I calculated that we would change roughly seven thousand diapers in the coming year, would prepare enough infant formula to float a small ship, discard enough baby food jars to cobble half the streets in the village. Imprisoned by our progeny, we left the house only to replenish rapidly diminishing supplies, wondering, as we glimpsed a world beyond babies, what had become of the life we once led, of movies and restaurants and languid Sunday mornings, of time to simply sit and think and sleep.

So haggard did we become that one well-meaning but hopelessly impolitic cashier once asked me if all those cartons of diapers and cases of baby food were for my grandchildren. "Grandchildren!" I all but shouted, turning to the woman behind me in line. "Do I look like a grandfather?" It took hours to calm me down and months to efface the sting. But a quick glance at the mirror told the tale. I had aged twenty years in as many days, days so wearying, so relentless that I often wondered how I would ever reach the end of the week, let alone survive the next few years. Would there ever come a time without this vast daily accumulation of laundry, of overflowing diaper pails, of baby bottles and pacifiers and frantic late-night calls to the pediatrician; would the day ever dawn when our every thought didn't turn to the care and feeding of children? I felt certain it wouldn't, that this state of abject infant dependency would last forever.

But, of course, I was mistaken. Somewhere in that great thicket of mind-numbing chores, that chaos of provisional parenting, the last diaper was finally removed and discarded, the final bottle given, the pacifier set aside and forgotten, the last baby food jar opened, emptied, and deposited in the recycling bin. And somewhere in all that activity, the last bedtime story was told, the last check under the bed for monsters, the last return for "one more hug." Longer ago than I can now recall, I hung the last of my children's wet bathing suits and towels over the lawn chairs to dry, washed their sandy hair, tied their shoes, buttoned their coats, zipped them into snow pants, made their last school lunch, told them to look both ways before crossing the street, fished through my pockets for the last quarter for bubble gum, the last dollar for ice cream. During those years I thought I would never see the end of macaroni art projects, Thanksgiving turkey hand tracings, construction paper alphabets, parent-teacher conferences; never leave off walking them to school and picking them up again at 3:00, never cease standing at the kitchen window watching them negotiate the street on the way to neighbors, never finish driving them to play dates, birthday parties, soccer games; never stop telling them to drink their milk, brush their teeth, wash their faces. But in time I stopped it all, and now, of course, I miss it—even those diapers.

We celebrate the great transitions of life, graduations from grade school, high school, and college, the figurative putting aside of childish things at Bar/Bat Mitzvah and Confirmation, the sea change of marriage, childbirth, new employment. But generally we are better at marking beginnings than endings, more mindful at the start of some new endeavor than its conclusion, preferring to look ahead rather than behind. Endings tend to be fuzzier. Most often it simply isn't in our power to know that we are standing upon a moment of transition, that the tide has turned beneath our feet, ebbing now instead of flowing. Surely I would not have leaned over red-faced with exasperation at having to switch the shoes on my daughter's feet yet again if I had known that this would be the last time, that somehow, miraculously, from that moment on, she would no longer need me to right her shoes or tie them. I would not have responded to my son's call to tuck him in with a somewhat reluctant, "I'll be up in a minute," if I had known that he would stop calling me to his room for a story and a kiss goodnight after that evening, that the next time I would read to him he would be in high school struggling over a passage of Shakespeare. But I did not know any more than I knew the last time I cut their meat for them, buttered their toast, poured their milk.

When the sage was asked how we should best live our lives, he replied, as though each day were to be our last. How much more attentive we would then be to every detail, every blessing, every wonder. Those diapers may not have seemed much of a prize back when three howling, wet-bottomed children demanded to be changed and we stood over them stupefied with exhaustion, but how dear that time seems in retrospect, how blessed with simple infant neediness. Would I want to revisit those years? No, I don't think so. But to have been mindful of the moment that last diaper was removed and the changing bag set in a corner never to be returned to service—that milestone I would have celebrated. So too tying my daughter's shoes one final time, brushing her tangled hair, buttoning her coat.

Our days are filled with endings, most of which we give scant thought to except in retrospect. What ever became of that restaurant we used to frequent, that TV show never missed, that treasured novel read and reread? When was the last time we called that old friend, saw that distant relative, that former neighbor? We mark the great leave-takings, the predictable conclusions in everyone's journey, but most other endings go unremarked. If only we knew then what we know now, that henceforth all small fingers would find their own way into mittens, spoons into mouths, toes into shoes. But we don't and we can't. And perhaps it's just as well. For the problem with living as the sage recommends is that the intensity of celebration, of perpetual gratitude, of a hyperawareness of life's blessings leads to utter exhaustion. We can't live at such a fever pitch for long without emotional collapse. After the anniversary or birthday celebration, the holiday rich with thanksgiving, we're spent; we need time to recover, seeking respite in the mundane and the mindless, returning to routine, losing ourselves in the petty details of the everyday. In retrospect, however, even those details will seem precious.

Long before we had children of our own, I watched a close friend negotiate the daily challenges of parenthood. Repeatedly I remarked on his willingness to be inconvenienced in the service of his children well after they were old enough to fend for themselves, driving them places they could easily walk or ride bikes to, preparing lunches they could make themselves. The day of their independence would dawn soon enough, he wistfully remarked. He was in no hurry to see them leave the nest emotionally or physically.

With one child in college and the other two aching to join her, it's too late to celebrate the many small milestones of childhood, but the twins still have a few weeks before they get their driving permits. They don't ask for rides very often these days but when they do I no longer begrudge the interruption, eager to spend a little time alone with them and find out what's new in their busy lives. All too soon this too will pass, a ride to the mall or to some friend's house proving, in retrospect, to have been the last. Will I know it when it happens? Probably not. But I'll have enjoyed those rides. And when, God-willing, grand-children come along, I'll be more mindful of the simple privilege of nurturing. But that's a natural condition of grandparenthood, I'm told. By the second time around we all realize how blessed we are simply to witness the daily miracles that fill our lives.

HEARTACHE AND DELIGHT

In the final hours of his long life, my grandfather began to hallucinate. Lying semi-comatose in Lenox Hill hospital on the upper east side of Manhattan, worlds away from the village of his birth, he started muttering to himself in Ladino, the ancient language of Sephardic Jewry, a language he had not spoken in sixty years.

He had been born almost eighty-five years earlier in Macedonia, a fertile, tobacco-growing region of northern Greece that had been ruled by the Ottoman Turks during his childhood. As a boy he had first learned the ancient language of his ancestors—Jewish refugees from Spain—a language the Inquisition had disseminated to North Africa, southern France, Italy, and eventually Greece, where his rabbinic ancestors settled in the late seventeenth century. Along with Ladino, he had been schooled in the modern Greek of his home town of Kavalla, as well as the Turkish of Constantinople, where he briefly attended medical school. But the overthrow of the last Sultan by the Young Turks in 1908 and their efforts to impress young Jews into their revolutionary army led to the first of his many dislocations. Before his peripatetic life came to a end, he would carry Greek, Turkish, German, Italian, French, and finally American passports and learn to communicate comfortably in as many languages.

Sitting by his hospital bed that last day of his life, my mother leaned toward his muttering lips in an effort to decipher his voiceless murmurings. Her father had always been so immaculately groomed, capable—even during his brief imprisonment by the Gestapo—of maintaining his dignity, shoes defiantly shined, tie knotted, suit brushed, hair closely trimmed. Until this final hospitalization she had never seen him unshaven, rarely even seen him in bed. He had always been the first up, the first out the door, returning each morning of her childhood with fresh bread and cheese just as she and my grandmother were rising. But since an unexplained fall three weeks earlier, he had not left his bed and, during his last days, had grown so restive that the nurses had not been able to shave him, allowing a coarse white stubble to overspread his cheeks and chin like frost.

It pained my mother to see him like that. What had become of the dignified cosmopolite who spoke eight languages, the man who passionately collected books, who abstained from gossip, never uttering an unkind word about another, not even after being hounded across the whole of Europe by Hitler's henchmen, who loved opera and bridge and crossing the Atlantic each summer by steamer to visit his only child and her four sons in New York? As she made out the tortured word that kept bubbling up from his unconscious, she realized that this dying man was not the father who had raised her, this was the child that had fathered the man, the child that had lain all but unacknowledged for more than three-quarters of a century, dormant but very much alive and still longing for the consolation he had never and could never receive. Now, as he slipped toward death, that desperate, lifelong need reasserted itself with all the power of infant love and loss, hoping this one last time to discover a different ending to the story, a more benign conclusion to the central trauma and tragedy of his life.

Many who write for children discover sooner or later that they are not writing for other children so much as for the child within, for a living, breathing, still enormously influential, largely unruly infant ego and its magical conception of the world. Somewhere early in their careers they realize that nothing provides quite as much pleasure as the act of making contact with that infant ego, of reentering the world of the child with its simple hierarchies of desire and its complex divisions of the forbidden. It isn't only the familiar landscapes of bygone years that attract them, but the emotional vigor of those memories, a vigor that seems confined to a time not of innocence so much as simple unknowing.

When I consider in the abstract what draws me to this writing life, the same word bubbles up through my own consciousness—delight: delight in allowing the simple play of the imagination to guide my thoughts and my pen, delight in the spinning of tales, delight in seeing the world with the freshness and wonder of a child, delight in taking up the cudgels for the deracinated and misunderstood eight-year-old boy that still lives so potently within. Watch virtually any child set loose in a room of non-descript objects—a cardboard box, an old glove, a scrap of paper, a broken shell—and you'll witness magic, caves and castles built from a tissue of words, peopled with knights and knaves, guided by secret maps to buried treasure. You'll overhear medical and mechanical experiments, rites and resurrections, the declaration and conquest of fears, simple ego gratifications, and superego admonishments. Children do not play to satisfy others—one has only to recall Miss Havisham's imperious command to Pip, "Play!" to know that no child ever truly played for the sake of another—children play for their own amusement and delight, for need and comfort and reassurance. But mostly they play to impose their understanding of the world—such as it is—back upon it, to test their growing sense of its complexities in an effort to keep it under their control and within their grasp.

The process of growth involves a gradual relinquishing of the enchanted constructs of childhood, the magical thinking that prescribes order, confers power, and wards off evil. One moment there was just mommy and me and my stomach. And then, suddenly, annoyingly, there was little brother and nursery school, there were clowns and ghosts, telephones and radios, streets not to be crossed and stairs that posed a grave and constant threat. There were rules and restrictions, reprimands and restraints. And there were untold miracles and mysteries. It may be an imperfect understanding of cause and effect, but it is organic and vital and comforting. And, in truth, we are all children attempting to construct a model of the universe that abides by the grace of heart and mind and answers to the moral imperatives that guide and sustain us.

As writers for children, our constructs may be more or less complicated, depending on our own lights. For some of us, moral ambiguity comes into sharper focus when we address an audience of children, for others that ambiguity all but vanishes. But what seems not to vary at all is the need to order the universe, to make it emotionally and intellectually cohesive, whether in tragedy or joy, positing a God of compassion in a cosmos of high risk, heartbreaking loss, and irretrievable innocence. Something in reader and writer alike cries out for justice in literary and dramatic forms. The inherent organicity of the literary process ordains that in our beginning shall be our end, that the fruits of our journey lie dormant in the seeds of our creation.

We are not free to go anywhere we choose, the writer quickly discovers: the way has been determined by the very first words of our tale. And in abiding by that simple law of nature, as it were, by watering root and leaf from the same source, our work derives its power and its ability to survive out in the world.

Consider my favorite children's story, the one that first got me thinking about the writing life when it was read to me at the age of eight back in 1960. That book, *Charlotte's Web*, was exactly as old as I was, barely eight years in print and already a classic. (I read recently that it continues to sell in excess of 100,000 copies annually, fifty-one years after publication. How many of us are that robust at fifty-one?) I'm sure I'm not the only one who can recite the book's first line from memory:

> *"Where's Papa going with that ax?" said Fern to her mother as they were setting the table for breakfast.*

In that simple, interrogatory opening lies all that is to follow, the whole enchanted story, beginning, middle and end, a death sentence imposed, a moral code invoked, the sentence stayed. By the end of the first page we learn the basic plot. A litter of pigs has just been born, including one so small and weak that "it will never amount to anything," according to Fern's mother, Mrs. Arable. "So your father has decided to do away with it," she adds. "'Do away with it?' shrieked Fern. 'You mean kill it? Just because it's smaller than the others?'"

You can't be a lover of words and not fall instantly in love with Fern and with E.B. White for that delicious puncturing of a mother's protective euphemism. As Alison Lurie pointed out more than a decade ago, the best of children's literature is subversive, challenging the status quo, granting young readers the warrant to question their received universe. Fern sets out to do just that and scores an important coup by the end of the second page. The runt of the litter will not be slaughtered but turned over to her care, and from that success grows not only the story that follows but the larger and more troubling issue that the spider Charlotte must confront long after Fern has all but evaporated from the tale in a stunning slight of hand that only White could have accomplished: how does one interrupt or alter the natural farm cycle, how change the destiny of the story's central character when to do so is to upset the very rhythms that underlie rural life?

Wilbur, a spring pig, has come into existence for only one reason, to become Christmas dinner? Not even Fern questions this destiny. She has convinced her father to prevent Wilbur's "untimely end," but with a pig's timely end, no one has taken issue, that is until Charlotte comes along. And then, in the great tradition of literary subversion, that end is drawn into question and Charlotte succeeds in saving a life and turning an entire community and its routines on its head. And she does so through the use of nothing more dramatic than a handful of web-written words (how the word "web" resonates for us today—if only White had lived to witness the enormous power of the worldwide web). The story's inevitable trajectory is determined, if not by the end of the first sentence, certainly by the end of the first page. Fern asks about an ax in the first line. It was Chekhov who reminded us that a pistol in scene one must be discharged by the last act. So, too, someone must die in Fern's world. But it's not Wilbur, of course, it's Charlotte, and she dies not through human intervention, but in the fullness of time, wholly consigned to her fate. We love *Charlotte's Web* because of its supreme naturalness. That may be an odd remark about a book in which animals talk like humans and spiders embroider words into their webs, but the patient and observant farmer that authored the book was true to the natural rhythms of the world he depicted, celebrating the cycle of life not as manipulated by man but as ordained by nature.

I've often wondered if the great naturalist and writer, Henry Beston, author of *The Outermost House, The St. Lawrence, Herbs and the Earth*, and *Northern Farm*, among other volumes, ever met E.B. White. They would have appreciated the keen eye each had for the telling natural detail, for their mutual love of contemplative solitude, and for the rocky coastline of Maine. White wrote his books and essays holed up in a small boathouse at the edge of his saltwater farm in Brooklin, Maine, one eye fixed upon the islanded waters of Southwest Harbor, the other upon the interior landscape of the imagination. Beston cultivated his herb garden a bit further south on the shores of Damariscotta Lake, writing his finely composed prose in the herb attic under the eaves of his ancient farmhouse. Though he wrote a handful of children's stories, none attained the stature of White's or Beston's wife, the children's author Elizabeth Coatsworth, but White would have nodded in agreement if he read in *Herbs and the Earth* that "It is only when we are aware of the earth and of the earth as poetry that we truly live," and more telling still, "True humanity is no inherent right but an achievement." Think of the many complex achievements that go into the humanizing of the characters in *Charlotte's Web*, plot complications, to be sure, but more importantly the labor of compassion.

Beston, in *The Outermost House*, that magnificent short chronicle of his year in a cabin amid the Cape Cod dunes, wrote "Nature is a part of our humanity, and without some awareness and experience of that divine mystery man ceases to be man." Blessed with almost infinite resources of patience, he seemed capable, quite literally, of watching his garden grow. His wife once wrote of his labors in the herb garden, "Henry, dressed in his oldest working clothes, would go out to sit beside the border staring down at it. At long intervals he might crumble a piece of earth between his fingers, or pull up a weed. But mostly he was just staring and staring. When he came in, he would say, 'I've been working in the herb garden all morning.'" And he had been, doing the hard labor of the writer, putting into language what, until that moment, had been only unvoiced observation, unremarked miracle. "Poetry is as necessary to comprehension as science," he wrote. "It is as impossible to live without reverence as it is without joy."

Beston's little classic is a celebration of the delight he took in discovery, the discovery of his neighbors, of seabirds and fish, of sand and wind and oceans and stars. The subject of his several books is the very stuff of life. Like White, he drew strength and inspiration from the natural world he actively cultivated, creating works that endure and delight, works that open our eyes and awaken our reverence.

And that, for me, is what children's literature is all about, an intoxication with life. So much of what we come to appreciate in life we come to know through the written word. For many of us, Bible stories are our first introduction not only to narrative but to an awareness of the world and its manifold mysteries. Noah alerts us to the sublimity of rainbows, the cleansing terror of floods, the saving grace of a carpenter's hands, the implications of a single, dove-borne olive leaf, the existence of evil, of righteousness, of forgiveness, of God. Who can listen to the story of Adam and Eve and ever look at an apple the same way afterwards? Or follow Charlotte's exploits and ever look at a spider the same way again? Stories sharpen our vision, deepen our appreciation, charge every little thing with significance. Writers are the map makers of the human soul, tracing to both source and the sea every rivulet and runnel of feeling, thought, and action; every aspiration, hope, and dread. They chronicle the adventure of life and help us bridge the terrible abyss that separates self from self.

I often ask my youngest students, can we ever truly know what it feels like to be another, to "walk around in another's shoes," as the saying goes? Even the most empathic among us can never make that great leap from the self to another. But pick up a book and the process is almost instantaneous. If you want to know what it feels like, truly feels like, to be a young girl in hiding from the Nazis in war-torn Holland, then read *The Diary of Ann Frank*; to feel what it's like to be a poor boy growing up on a hardscrabble farm in rural Florida, read *The Yearling;* an orphan in London, read *Oliver Twist;* cast adrift by a mentally-ill mother in modern-day New England with three younger siblings, no money, no food, no father, read *Homecoming*. We all try to bridge the gap between the self and others through movies; it's our national pastime. But cinema, in all but a few gifted hands, never quite accomplishes what whole libraries of books are capable of: a genuine out-of-body experience that transports the reader to another place, another life, another realm of feeling and thought. If we are most human in those moments when we truly empathize with others, leaping across the abyss that divides self from self, then it is literature that best facilitates that leap as no other art form.

And if it is transporting for the reader, how much more so for the writer. What is it that draws us, day after day, year after year, to sit staring at our own thoughts, spinning webs of words from our own *kishkas* (as my father used to say), our own essence, sitting from sunrise to sunset and often well into the night in boating sheds and attics, at kitchen tables and desks, in living rooms and libraries, windowless offices and the great outdoors? Why do we squander the precious minutes of our all-too-brief time here on earth staring at computer screens and blank sheets of paper? What is so important about transcribing our thoughts that vast armies of scribblers, myself among them, can think of no more meaningful way to spend their lives than in writing?

How can I make this clear? It's somewhat in the realm of, "If you've got to ask, you'll never understand." My children certainly don't. They always choose the movie over the book, forgoing both for the music video or, better yet, some profanity-laced rap CD. How can you sit there, day after day, they ask me, doing the same thing? But it's not the same thing, I insist. One day it may be poetry, another day short stories, on a third I'm wrestling with a novel or an essay, or simply updating my journal. The landscape changes as rapidly as the subject. The day is spent aloft, touring the cosmos. Is it any wonder I'm forever dreaming of flight?

Despite their bewilderment at my choices, I think my children find it a comfort, regardless of whether or not they understand the motivation, grateful for the stability and contact this writing life has provided. I bless the written word for so many reasons, not the least of which is the close proximity it has allowed me to maintain with my family. I have written within earshot of them since my oldest was newborn nineteen years ago, watching them with an author's eye for the subtle cohesions of childhood and youth, the wonderful unities of siblings, the traceries of their inheritance, a great-grandfather's forehead, a grandmother's eyes, a father's temper, a mother's artistry. Unless we look for it, it too often goes unnoticed.

"Did Mama sing every day?" asked Caleb. "Every-single-day?"...He pushed his chair back. It made a hollow scraping sound on the hearthstones....

Recognize the opening? Patricia MacLachlan's *Sarah, Plain and Tall,* a book about the music of the soul and the hollowness of the heart after a great loss and the power of nature to fill that hollow and heal that heart. Here, too, the story's inevitable trajectory is contained within the opening words. Perhaps I mislead you by suggesting that this all comes about alchemically. Of course it doesn't, it's the product of great patience and innumerable revisions, but it's also the result of the deep connections that words forge in and of themselves.

Whenever I find myself casting about for direction in the midst of a story, I return to the beginning, confident that I'll find my way hidden in the reeds of its inception. When my students tell me they're blocked, I urge them to trust the process, to pay close attention to the words themselves, to the ideas and images they evoke, to the seemingly random play of the imagination. It's a ludic endeavor we're engaged in, playful, ludicrous, perhaps even lunatic. Shakespeare stated it most succinctly, "The lunatic, the lover, and the poet, are of imagination all compact," we hear voices and respond to them following a logic that is not always of this world but rather impelled by the mysterious workings of the unconscious. To those who insist they are suffering writer's block, I tell them what others have said and I firmly believe: that writer's block is nothing more than a failure of the ego, the sudden collapse of the will, the loss of the conviction that stories matter, that thought matters, that one person speaking to the world matters even if, at the moment, no one seems to be listening.

The great delight for the writer is the slow unfolding of this process, the companionship that the unconscious provides, telegraphing intent long before we know it ourselves, speaking in tongues, in unanticipated characters, in hieroglyphics that slowly reveal the preoccupations of the psyche. Before the first word has been put to paper the die is cast, our course is set. We need merely follow along, allowing the imagination to do its dreamwork. Listen again to what Shakespeare says:

> The poet's eye, in a fine frenzy rolling,
> Doth glance from heaven to earth, from earth to heaven;
> And, as imagination bodies forth
> The forms of things unknown, the poet's pen
> Turns them to shapes, and gives to airy nothing
> A local habitation and a name.

To airy nothing a local habitation and a name: That is what we do, and in doing so create worlds that the world finds more real, more compelling than reality, more engaging than the office, the factory, the schoolyard, indeed, sometimes, the home.

We know Willa Cather's Red Cloud better than we know our own local villages and cities. We know it so intimately we go in search of it.

Not far from my home, the town of North Tarrytown recently renamed itself for the fictional village America's first great popular writer situated there on the banks of the Hudson River, Sleepy Hollow. Ride through the village today and you'll encounter street corners festooned with flags depicting the Headless Horseman. In France the village of Illiers renamed itself Illiers-Combray, taking the name conferred by its most illustrious son, Marcel Proust, not merely as a way of paying homage, but out of the simple commercial desire to capitalize on the reader's impulse to visit the local habitation the writer has named.

What writer of fiction has not been asked to identify his sources, to provide the real identities lurking behind his pseudonymous creations, the real place names of the cities, towns, and villages constructed out of thin air? Give the constructs of the imagination an identity, place them in some dream location, and the congress of readers will attempt to locate that imaginary town on a map of the known world. Knowing this, William Faulkner drew a map of his fictive Yoknapatawpha County, Mississippi, complete with roads, villages, and population figures. Ever since, entire literary conferences and scholarly tomes have been devoted to parsing that county as though its inhabitants were something more than simply the inspired imaginings of a regional writer with a taste for bourbon. Visitors to London go in search of Little Nell's Old Curiosity Shop, the Eaton Place townhouse of the Bellamys of *Upstairs, Downstairs* fame, the old blacking factory of *David Copperfield*, even Harry Potter's track 9 3/4 at King's Cross Station, as if to do so, to find evidence of such places, will somehow reify these creatures of the imagination, conferring life upon them like latter-day Pinocchios or Pygmalions, giving us the right to celebrate and to mourn them as though they had truly lived and, moreover, lived for us.

And we explore the very neighborhoods our favorite writers walked, visiting Emily Dickenson's Amherst gardens and sparsely furnished rooms, the Sunnyside haunts of Washington Irving, Thoreau's Walden pond, Hawthorne's Salem, Emerson's Concord, Melville's Manhattan and Pittsfield, hoping for a glimpse of that which inspired great and lasting art and a deeper understanding of its sources. The world seems so much more vibrant through the eyes of our artists. Ansel Adams has probably brought more tourists to Yosemite National Park than Half Dome itself. Van Gogh connoisseurs flock to Arles, John Constable fans to Salisbury Cathedral, Monet devotees to Giverny. All of us awaken to the world through the eyes and words of great artists. And the artist himself long ago discovered that he is most alive to the world, most receptive to its manifold miracles, when he is creatively responsive to it. Which is why so many writers write and painters paint and musicians perform regardless of their audience, filling notebooks with unread stories, sketchbooks with unseen drawings, empty rooms with song. They do so because only then do they feel most vital, most responsive to the promptings of their soul. Actors are known as "players," but all artists are players, all engaged in the meaningful play of life, attempting to order our complex and bewildering world.

But dedicating one's life to this endeavor is no guarantee that the world will reciprocate one's interest. Perhaps the hardest lesson for young artists to learn is that the world does not owe them a living. Never mind a living, it does not even owe them a hearing. It is the nature of the writer's task to work in isolation, looking inward, listening and studying the private promptings of the heart. Some, like Hemingway, are able to conduct that discourse in the midst of noisy cafés, but most seek the quiet of empty rooms or hushed libraries where they are better able to hear those inner voices. We pay a price for this isolation, removing ourselves from the world even as we attempt to engage it. In order to be most alive to the world, to represent it in all its staggering multiplicity, we need to stand apart, analyzing its effect upon us. Weeks, months, sometimes years pass. We do our work and then return to the world bearing our gifts of interpretation. But does the world need or want these gifts? Does it even know such gifts exist?

When I visit elementary schools I often ask the students to guess how many new titles are published in America each year. Some say ten books, some ten million. Neither they nor I can truly grasp what the real number means: somewhere between forty and fifty thousand new titles annually! What are we to make of such a flood of thought? Consider how many books you bought for your personal use in the last twelve months; consider too that most American families don't buy more than a book or two a year and most of those will belong to the narrow category, best-seller—books that have earned the right to catch your eye the moment you enter the chain bookstore or warehouse supermarket. But what of the rest of them, of the thousands of books each year that are never reviewed outside of trade publications, if at all, that are never advertised, never even shelved in bookstores, or shelved for a scant few weeks before being returned? Our perception of the book world is skewed by the success stories that occasionally make headlines: the J.K. Rowlings phenomenon that has eight year olds reading breathlessly through 870 pages of adventure alongside their grateful parents, the first novel that sells for untold millions, the octogenarian poet signed for six figures. These are wonderful developments for their authors, but they mask the true state of publishing today.

I don't want to dwell on the heartache of this process, but having spoken of the delight that underlies the impulse to write, I would be guilty of speaking in half truths if I failed to acknowledge the heartache of the birthing process, the heartache of the aftermath. Sooner or later most writers discover the simple fact that the world will neither survive nor perish as a result of their labors, that, in fact, the world could not care less whether they ever write another word. With fifty thousand new books being published annually, who needs another? It's an agonizing truth, especially after one has devoted a year or two to teasing a reluctant vision from the ether, only to discover that it has "no market," as publishers like to say.

Rub two writers together and within minutes they'll combust, their heated conversation turning to the deplorable state of publishing today, the death of independent bookstores, the swallowing up of dedicated smaller publishers by rapacious conglomerates, the eclipse of the art of editing, the slow strangulation of the mid-list author, the plague of remaindering, the absence of advertising dollars—in short, the imminent collapse of the literary world as we know it or wish it to be. The sad fact is that this seems always to have been the case, at least for those who find themselves out of the literary loop. Maxwell Perkins has been dead more that fifty years and still one is likely to overhear laments that the publishing world has never recovered from the loss of his dedication to both the craft of writing and to the emotional well-being of his authors.

There was a time, writers like to believe, roughly coterminous with Perkins' tenure at Scribners, when publishers took a paternal interest in their authors, supporting them financially and emotionally, nurturing and encouraging them, taking the lesser along with the greater works in benevolent understanding of the fragile psyche of the artist; a time when editors truly edited, taking their lunches not at The Four Seasons and Le Cirque in the company of agents but at their desks with sharpened pencils at their elbows. Perkins never left the office without a briefcase overflowing with manuscripts that occupied his every evening and weekend. Editors today seem to lose interest in a manuscript the moment the deal is closed, moving on to the next prospect, leaving the laborious business of text to the copy editing department.

From my limited perspective, having been on the receiving end of both dedicated and indifferent editors, I can report that the state of publishing is probably as sanguine as ever, with examples abounding of both its shortcomings and virtues. I cast no blame, offer no solutions. Publishing has always struggled against the inherent uncertainties of the industry, locked in a love-hate relationship with the very imponderables that attract so many to it. Who knows but that the next million seller might come over the transom this morning, the brilliant brainchild of some unknown visionary. Who knows but that the great expectations of editor, publisher, and author might be met by an apathetic and parsimonious public. Like all business executives, publishers seek certainties. Cook books provide such certainties, so, too, self-help books, proven bestselling authors, Hollywood celebrities, recent presidents and their spouses, and almost anyone associated with scandal. When criticized for glutting a saturated market with more of the same, the industry reminds us that such certainties pay the bills and provide the small profit margin that allows them to take chances with unknown authors and so-called literary writers (painful to think how many non-literary writers are out there).

How have I fared in this environment: better than some, worse than others. I have written roughly ten manuscripts for every one that I've published; have published no more than four books with any one house or editor; have had editors vanish in midstream, leaving my books orphaned in the midst of publication, my publishers swallowed whole, my books remaindered, my latest submissions returned unread after a year on someone's slush pile. Not long ago I called one of my former publishers to check on the status of a manuscript. Since submitting the work, my original editor had left to join another house, the publisher had been replaced, and the house itself had been purchased by a European conglomerate. I eventually found myself speaking to the executive editor who, on hearing my name, asked if I had published a short story recently in a particular magazine. I told her I had. "Isn't this a coincidence," she remarked. "Just yesterday I walked into my publisher's office, showed her your story and said, 'We ought to publish his work.' And here you are calling me the very next day!"

"How did your publisher react to your suggestion?" I asked.

"She seemed enthusiastic."

"Did she recognize my name?" I wondered aloud.

"Should she have?" the editor asked.

"Well, I don't know. I believe you're still publishing three of my titles."

"We already publish you?" she asked, dismayed. "Well, I'm embarrassed."

She needn't have been. Only one of those three books, I soon learned, was still in print, the other two remaindered as soon as the house was bought and new management brought in to "streamline the list." And so it goes.

The longer I write the more difficult it is to get into print. And the longer I write the less important it becomes to do so. Samuel Johnson famously opined that "No man but a blockhead wrote but for money," and in our commercially driven world, it's hard to argue with that sentiment. But Emily Dickenson, cherished muse of the unknown and the unpublished, examples a very different course, a course that seeks validation not through the marketplace but the heart, that owes its success or failure not to commercial imperatives but artistic ones, that emerges into the light suckled by private passion not popularity. The image of her filling her handsewn packets with poem after unread poem, as many as three hundred in some years, nearly 1,800 in all, only to deposit those sixty-odd packets in an attic trunk all but unread, leaves one both exhilarated and disheartened: exhilarated by her perseverance, by her devotion to art, and depressed by the world's stunning indifference to her genius. The only editorial notice or advice she ever received was so famously wrong-headed that it does us well to keep it in mind when tempted to despair by the responses of modern editors. Thomas Wentworth Higginson, the eventual editor of the first posthumous volumes of her poetry, told the young, inquiring Emily that her verse was "remarkable, though odd…not strong enough to publish," that her metrics were spasmodic, her rhymes imperfect, the whole presentation uncontrolled. She stoically replied: "If fame belonged to me, I could not escape her—if she did not, the longest day would pass me on the chase—and the approbation of my Dog, would forsake me—then. My Barefoot Rank is better." It is the rare artist who can sustain herself wholly in isolation, who can maintain that life-affirming dialogue between the soul and society without society's response. Promethean as we would like to view ourselves, most writers long to be read, and not merely read but praised. The sad truth at the core of this business is that few who write will be published, few of those published read, fewer still understood and appreciated. Yet we keep at it, pursuing that lunatic hope.

And now and again comes a day like the one I enjoyed a decade ago when my firstborn child was turning ten. For most of her young life we had read together, enjoying a nightly ritual of story-telling that imprinted us both in ways we are only just now beginning to understand and appreciate. In the beginning, Elizabeth lay across my lap more intent on sucking the book in my hands than on the words she was hearing, but gradually she began to listen and then to repeat back from memory the tales she heard, holding the volume as though reading it herself, even turning the pages at the appropriate moment. And then, miraculously, she cracked the code and became a reader herself, sounding out words as she sat beside me, her finger moving slowly across the page, appropriating a whole new language, a whole new life. She still enjoyed being read to, to lie back against my chest and drift with the currents of the narrative, but increasingly we began to alternate—first sentences, then pages, then chapters—our story hour a shared enterprise of reading and listening, giving and receiving.

By fifth grade Elizabeth was competing with her classmates to see who could read the most books by the time they graduated from elementary school that June. Armed with a long list of children's classics, she brought two or three new titles home every week and together, sitting cross-legged on her bed, we read them aloud. For her it was a time of great enchantment, her first encounter with the likes of *Charlotte's Web, The Secret Garden, The Wind in the Willows, Sarah, Plain and Tall.* For me it was an opportunity to revisit the precincts of childhood fantasy in the company of my child, to receive those tales from her mouth, hear them told in her voice with an innocence and immediacy that had not been present the first time I read them.

I had begun by then to write my own stories, initially for adults but increasingly, as Elizabeth's voice seeped into my consciousness, in a language intended for her. The year of her great immersion in children's literature I put a newly published book of mine, *The Shadow Children*, in her hands and asked her to read it to me. I had revised the tale so often I knew it by heart but in all that time I had never heard the story recited in the voice of my narrator, a child my daughter's age. And until that moment I had not been able to gauge its accuracy or effectiveness, its appropriateness or vitality. But that night, in the same small voice that had given me back Louisa May Alcott and Hans Christian Andersen, Dr. Seuss, and A.A. Milne, I heard my own words as if for the first time and understood viscerally what it means for a work to come to life, for ideas and images to clothe themselves in the raiments of a child's imagination, animated by a child's curiosity as it is sung in the high, arresting treble of a child's voice. In that moment a work I had labored over for years took on a life of its own, set free to live independently in the world.

For that is where our books truly live, not in the minds of their authors but in the voices of children. We write from the perspective of adults hoping to capture the timbre of childhood, but we are vetted by adult agents, contracted by adult editors, distributed by adult booksellers, and purchased by parents and teachers. Only rarely do we get a chance to experience, independent of adult perceptions, the impact of our work on our intended audience. By a fortunate confluence of events, I was privileged to glimpse my audience and my narrator in the same person, my daughter. She read my story as she had so many others that year, forgetting by the second paragraph that her father had written the words. To her it was just another tale, another road to travel, another life to live. That she wanted to walk that road and inhabit that life several nights running was all the reward I could ever hope to reap from my words. In the litany of a writer's most memorable moments, it ranked very high indeed. On balance, the delights have far outweighed the heartaches.

And what of my grandfather, murmuring in Ladino on his deathbed. The word that kept bubbling up through his semi-consciousness was "burro," or donkey. A city dweller all his adult life, his only contact with donkeys had come early in his childhood in the mountains of Macedonia. Hearing that word and a few other mumbled expressions, my mother realized that in his final hours of life he was reliving an event that had taken place in 1888, in his third year, in the village of his birth. Only once had he mentioned it to her, perhaps as a cautionary tale, perhaps in an effort to expiate a sin for which he could never fully atone.

In his childhood an itinerant salesman used to visit his village several times a year, companioned by a donkey heavily ladened with dry goods: bolts of cloth, pots and pans, colorful trinkets, toys, sweets. The clanging, tinkling, flamboyantly arrayed animal drew all the neighborhood children to its flanks as it proceeded down the dusty main street of the village. Behind all the children, clamoring for sweets and a chance to ride high atop the donkey's load, came mothers with knives to be sharpened and pans to be repaired, with orders for needles and thread, for fabric and ribbons, paper and pens. My three-year-old grandfather was forbidden to leave the front yard unaccompanied by his mother, but the circus atmosphere of the itinerant peddler overcame this injunction one spring morning. Unwatched for a moment, he bolted from the garden and joined the throng.

An hour passed, clouds moved across the sky, and a cold rain began to fall. The peddler gathered up his wares and ambled out of town in search of shelter, putting up for the night in an abandoned barn. My grandfather, still mesmerized by the donkey, followed him, taking cover in the barn during the worst of the storm. By then his young mother had discovered his absence and gone in frantic search for him, tearing through the village shouting for her only child, oblivious to the drenching rain. By the time she found him, dry and unharmed, she had begun to shiver from the cold. She took to her bed soon after, and, as my grandfather later told my mother, never again left it, succumbing to pneumonia. All his life he had lived with the guilt of his mother's death and in his final moments returned to his village, hoping perhaps for a different outcome or, at the very least, for forgiveness.

Though we think we outgrow childhood disappointments, believing that adulthood is an altogether different realm, I suspect we spend our adult lives orbiting the sun of our youth, its great gravitational force continuing to motivate and determine so many of our actions and choices. Among writers for children, that core is perhaps more accessible, but it lives in us all as it continued to live in my grandfather. Until the day he died he hoped to be absolved of a death he was too young to be responsible for, yet felt burdened by all his life. His conscience burned with that guilt until his life was extinguished.

Are we writers all children of conscience? I believe so, though I would be hard-pressed to prove it. It strikes me as significant that we are able to suspend the laws of nature when we dream, but rarely the laws of morality. I regularly take flight as I sleep, defying gravity at will, soaring above the treetops. But I am not free to lie, to cheat, to commit adultery, even to dent an adjacent car in the supermarket parking lot without suffering pangs of guilt and awaking to a great sense of relief. Perhaps not all writers are driven by a sense of morality but those works that survive, that we return to generation after generation, are deeply moral, and upon them we construct our own moral universe.

Writing, for me, has always been an expression of gratitude, an outgrowth of the impulse to give thanks for love received, for children born, for the miraculous existence of the imagination, for the simple facts of the natural world. When I write for adults, I often do so in a state of wonder, transfixed by blessings. When I write for children, I try to recapture the eight-year-old boy I once was, a boy filled with passionate interest in the world just beginning to unfold around him. And I write in the hope of leaving behind a legacy of thought and feeling that my children might one day mine, if not for answers at least for solace in the recognition that we traveled the same road of doubt and discovery, encountering many of the same challenges, the same glories, the same disappointments. In the end that's really all we do, give notice to the world of our inmost thoughts, reflecting the world back upon itself, its miracle and majesty, poetry and playfulness, the simple and sublime. And no one put the endeavor better than Emily Dickenson in one of her last poems. Returning to a kind of childhood memory in her final years, she wrote:

> *To make a prairie it takes a clover and one bee,*
> *One clover, and a bee,*
> *And revery.*
> *The revery alone will do,*
> *If bees are few.*

That, ultimately, is what we are all about, the reverie, and truly, it alone will do, if bees are few.

0-595-29577-0